Oxford International Primary

6

Science
Workbook

Deborah Roberts
Terry Hudson

Alan Haigh
Geraldine Shaw

Language consultants:
John McMahon
Liz McMahon

OXFORD

Great Clarendon Street, Oxford, OX2 6DP, United Kingdom

Oxford University Press is a department of the University of Oxford. It furthers the University's objective of excellence in research, scholarship, and education by publishing worldwide. Oxford is a registered trade mark of Oxford University Press in the UK and in certain other countries.

British Library Cataloguing in Publication Data

Data available

ISBN 978-1-382006651

5 7 9 10 8 6 4

Paper used in the production of this book is a natural, recyclable product made from wood grown in sustainable forests. The manufacturing process conforms to the environmental regulations of the country of origin.

Printed in China by Golden Cup

Acknowledgements

The publisher and authors would like to thank the following for permission to use photographs and other copyright material:

Cover: Artwork by Blindsalida. Photos: **p28(l):** Photononstop/Alamy Stock Photo; **p28(r):** Veaceslav Malai/Alamy Stock Photo; **p43:** James Porcini/Cultura/ Getty Images; **p62:** Ekaterina Minaeva/Alamy Stock Photo; **p70:** Najib Habib/ Shutterstock; **p75:** eFesenko/Alamy Stock Photo; **p77:** Classic Image/Alamy Stock Photo; **p80(l):** David Papazian/Shutterstock; **p80(r):** Naiyyer/Bigstock; **p82:** Anton Brehov/Shutterstock; **p85:** Alessandro de Leo/Shutterstock; **p103:** Nils Versemann/Shutterstock; **p108:** Oprea Nicolae/Alamy Stock Photo; **p114:** Peter Vanco/Shutterstock; **p139:** IanRedding/Shutterstock; **p143(l):** mariait/Shutterstock; **p143(r):** Neirfy/Shutterstock.

Artwork by Q2A Media Services Pvt. Ltd.

Every effort has been made to contact copyright holders of material reproduced in this book. Any omissions will be rectified in subsequent printings if notice is given to the publisher.

Contents

How to Use this Book

The Workbook for *Oxford International Primary Science* supports the Student Book that children are using in their science lessons for this year.

The Student Book includes some pair, group and whole-class activities, hands-on tasks and write-in tasks to test students' understanding and help them learn. It is important to extend these tasks. This Workbook enables students to build on what they have learned in the Student Book to develop a secure understanding of scientific concepts.

Encouraging students to think about and apply their growing skills and knowledge helps them consolidate their understanding and work scientifically. This helps with confidence. Students also have opportunities to see that science is relevant all around them – both inside and outside the classroom.

Students may find it useful to complete an investigation planning form. This sets out all the stages of the investigation. A proforma is provided in the Teacher's Guide. Find out more at:

www.oxfordprimary.com/international-science

Structure of the book

This Workbook is divided into five units plus a Support for Teachers and Parents section and a Quiz:

Support for Teachers and Parents
Unit 1 Classification and Habitats
Unit 2 Organs and Systems
Unit 3 The Way We See Things
Unit 4 Building Electrical Circuits
Unit 5 Adaptation and Inherited Characteristics
Quiz Yourself

What you will find in each unit

There are four types of lessons:

Key words and introduction lessons encourage students to read, spell and use the scientific vocabulary in the unit.

Activities build on the work in the Student Book. These help with developing language skills, developing scientific enquiry skills, applying mathematical knowledge and securing understanding rather than just recall. The Support for Teachers and Parents notes on pages 6–13 give you advice on how to help students with each activity.

What I have learned encourages students to talk about what they have learned, reflect on what went well and revisit any areas they need to check. This encourages a growth mindset.

Investigate like a scientist enables students to apply what they have learned in practical contexts.

What you will find in the lessons

Icons show the nature of each task:

Discuss: Students are encouraged to discuss and communicate scientific ideas and approaches. They can work in pairs or small groups for discussion tasks.

Investigate: Students are encouraged to plan, ask questions and record results for each investigation. They are asked to observe closely, make predictions and compare their results with others. Sometimes you will use different equipment, which is available in school. You may also ask students to carry out a test in a different way, to make sure they are safe.

Language support: This icon highlights activities that provide language support through writing frames or word banks. Students are encouraged to write, read and record short answers.

Hints and tips: Students are encouraged to think about tips to make investigations safer or more effective.

Stretch zone: Students are encouraged to extend their understanding.

Mindful moments: Students are encouraged to think about and reflect on what they have learned. This supports students' well-being.

What went well: Students are encouraged to talk about what went well in each module to secure their understanding.

Student Book

Throughout the Workbook, you will find links to the Student Book. Students can refer to information in the Student Book to help them complete activities.

Teacher's Guide

The Teacher's Guide that accompanies this book provides lesson notes and answers for each page.

Support for Teachers and Parents

1 Classification and Habitats

What students will learn

This unit helps students to understand more about living things and how they are classified into groups. They use the characteristics of living things to place them into the appropriate group. Students consider a range of habitats and look at the ways in which humans can care for and protect habitats, and how human activity can lead to the destruction of habitats and the animals and plants that live there. Students will:

- group living things using classification systems
- explore the reasons for classifying living things based on their characteristics
- explore how humans have positive (good) and negative (bad) effects on the environment
- learn about a number of ways of caring for the environment.

Key words

characteristic, classification, conservation, deforestation, environment, greenhouse effect, habitat, key, kingdom, microorganism, pollution, species

Scientific enquiry skills

This unit helps students to develop and practise the following scientific enquiry skills.

Scientific enquiry skill	Page
Plan and/or carry out enquiries to answer questions	17, 19–21, 25–26, 28–33, 38–39, 41
Make predictions	26, 32–33, 36, 41
Recognise and control variables	26, 30, 41
Make observations	17, 19–20, 22–23, 26, 28, 30, 33, 38, 41
Take measurements, using equipment accurately	19, 26, 30, 36, 41
Record data and results	17–21, 23, 26, 28, 30, 32–33, 35, 36, 39, 41
Analyse data, notice patterns and group or classify things	16, 19–20, 23, 26–27, 30, 32–33, 35–36, 38–39, 41
Report and present findings	16, 18–20, 23, 25–26, 29–31, 33, 36–39, 41
Draw conclusions and give explanations	19–20, 22–23, 25–30, 35–36, 38, 41
Identify causal relationships	19, 24, 26, 30, 36, 41

Ways to help

- Encourage students to observe the animals and plants in their local area.
- Display pictures of a range of different habitats in the room so students can observe them.
- Ask students to think about why it is important to care for habitats.
- Encourage students to use classification keys and identification books to find out the names of living things and group them.

Helping with activities

The following guidance gives you advice on how to help students with each activity.

Identifying the correct kingdom
Encourage students to have their Student Book open to help them to consider the characteristics of the various major groups.

Plant classification survey
Tell students that some of the plants will be very small. Remind them to use a hand lens to look for single-celled algae and mosses.

Classifying animals
Encourage students to think of two or three characteristics for each animal, and how the adaptation helps the animal to survive.

Different shaped beaks
Ask students to compare the type and number of seeds picked up by each tool. Let them think about how efficient each tool was.

Classifying local plants
Try to include some small pond plants – even microscopic – in the survey. Collect small amounts of water in small bottles.

Researching microorganisms
Arrange access to the internet to help with the research task. If this is not possible, download the information sheets yourself or have biology books available.

Making your own classification key
Remind students to design questions that have only a 'yes' or 'no' answer to help them to use the key.

Designing a classification key
Remind students that it is best to choose characteristics that are permanent and easy to identify. Colour and size are particularly problematic.

Protecting our environment
Explain that all of the words needed to fill the blank spaces will be found in the word box.

Conservation project

Collect information leaflets, posters and website information from local conservation groups. Consider inviting a speaker in to talk to students.

Investigate the greenhouse effect

Allow students to take the temperature inside the greenhouse at different times of the day.

The greenhouse effect

If students have problems with the labels, let them look back to page 27 of their Student Book for extra support.

Stone survey

Explain that even a stone that has been shaped or smoothed, or even cut into small pieces, should be included.

Deforestation debate

Explain to students that looking for flaws in the opposite side of an argument or idea is a useful way to understand an issue.

How cloudy is the water?

Point out to students that particles in the water will scatter and block light, so the dirtier the water the less clearly they will see the squares through it.

Waste disposal in the local area

Discuss that a waste material for one person may be useful for another, so many objects could be reused as well as being recycled.

Saving energy at home

Explain that there are different ways to measure the energy used by an appliance. Students can multiply the kilowatts used by the appliance by the length of time it is used for to get a useful measure of energy use.

School energy survey

Arrange a tour around the school that includes a wide range of appliances. Include larger appliances in a kitchen or workshop, for example.

Make a useful object from waste materials

Encourage students to be imaginative. Remind them not to copy any of the examples in their Student Book.

Interpreting recycling data

Remind students to look carefully at the axes of any charts and graphs they are interpreting so they know the categories, scale and numbers involved.

Litter survey

Explain that objects found that are a mixture of materials should be classified based on which material makes up most of the object.

Design an anti-litter poster

Consider having examples of posters available for display to enthuse students and give them new ideas.

Air pollution

Explain that the size of the holes in the filter materials will dictate the type of solid pollution that is trapped.

Saving energy questionnaire

Show students how to make a tally chart as they ask the questions, so they do not have to wait until the end to write a number in.

2 Organs and Systems

What students will learn

This unit helps students to understand more about organs and organ systems. They identify the major organs and locate where they are found in the body. Students learn about the circulatory system and how nutrients and water are moved around the body and kept in balance. They explore the importance of diet, exercise and other factors on health. Students will:

- learn where the major organs are to be found in the human body
- find out about the main functions of the major organs
- explore the human circulatory system and describe the functions of the heart, blood vessels and blood
- describe how nutrients and water are transported in humans and animals
- recognise how diet, exercise, drugs and lifestyle affect our bodies.

Key words

circulatory system, defence mechanism, digestive system, drug, function, infectious disease, lifestyle, medicine, nervous system, organ, urinary system, vaccine

Scientific enquiry skills

This unit helps students to develop and practise the following scientific enquiry skills.

Scientific enquiry skill	Page
Plan and/or carry out enquiries to answer questions	43, 49, 53, 55, 57, 59, 61–62, 64, 67
Make predictions	43
Recognise and control variables	43, 49, 53
Make observations	43, 45–46, 48–50, 53, 55–56, 59, 62, 67
Take measurements, using equipment accurately	43, 47, 49, 55, 57, 59
Record data and results	43–44, 47, 49, 53, 55, 57, 59, 61–64
Analyse data, notice patterns and group or classify things	43, 49, 55, 59, 62–64
Report and present findings	43–45, 47, 49, 53, 55–57, 59, 61, 63–64, 67
Draw conclusions and give explanations	43, 48–49, 51, 55–57, 59, 62–64
Identify causal relationships	43, 49, 51, 53, 55, 59

Ways to help

- Encourage students to keep a diary of the foods they eat.
- Display pictures and posters of the organ systems in the room so students can observe them.
- Ask students to review earlier work on heart rate and exercise.
- Encourage students to learn the names of the major organs and systems by displaying key words and terms.

Helping with activities

The following guidance gives you advice on how to help students with each activity.

Where are our organs?
Allow students to look back at their Student Book if they need clues about where to place the organs.

Tracing the organs
Demonstrate how to take a tracing if students are not familiar with the technique.

Our heart, lungs and brain
Point to the parts of the body where the relevant bones are located: the head (skull), the chest (ribs) and the chest bone (sternum).

Summary table
Explain that all of the words needed are in the word box. Suggest that students tick them off as they are used.

How we breathe
Talk through the breathing process as you make exaggerated breathing in and out actions.

Breathing rates
Make sure students are fully rested before starting the investigation, otherwise you will find elevated rates at the start.

Label the parts of the circulatory system
Help students to remember which vessels move blood to and from the heart by using the spelling of vein. It ends with 'in' and it takes blood 'in' to the heart.

Exercise, pulse rates and fitness
Remind students that pulse rates naturally vary between people, but exercise will always increase pulse rate.

Parts of the digestive system
Students can work through this activity as a class or in small groups if they need support labelling the diagram.

Breaking down food
Provide small mirrors so students can find the different types of teeth in their own mouth.

How nutrients enter the blood
You can illustrate the need to have nutrients broken down by asking students to think about how a large tent could be passed through a small window.

Investigating surface area and absorption
Demonstrate how to carry out the calculation and stress how folding allows a larger surface area to be fitted into a small space.

Model the function of the kidney
Use as big a space as possible. Make the holes in the cardboard just big enough for two types of ball (water and urea) to pass through, but not the balls representing protein, sugar and blood cells.

How the urinary system works
Stress that students should only use words from the word box to label the diagram and fill in the gaps.

The brain and nerves
Allow students to use their Student Book as a research resource to work out the answers to the questions.

How sensitive is your skin?
Demonstrate how to make the pointer and stress that the distance between the two points is vital and must be measured accurately.

Learning about microorganisms
Encourage students to write out the names of the main types of pathogens (viruses, bacteria, parasites and fungi) a few times to become familiar with them.

Researching diseases and pathogens
Provide access to the internet to help students find out about the pathogens or print out information for them.

Food labels survey

Provide as many types of food labels as possible as it will be useful for students to see the different ways in which food information is presented.

Make your own healthy eating plate

Point out that students may see different versions of the healthy eating plate. Every healthy eating plate will emphasise eating fruit and vegetables and not eating too much sugar and fat.

Exercise survey

Point out to students that numbers that are being counted or measured in an investigation are usually written up the Y-axis of a graph or chart.

Personal hygiene

Encourage students to reflect on their own personal hygiene practice, but keep this confidential by not engaging in class or group debate.

3 The Way We See Things

What students will learn

This unit helps students to understand more about light and how we see objects. They see that light travels in straight lines and review how objects are seen due to light reflecting from them and entering the eyes. Students look in detail at reflection and mirrors and investigate how the blocking of light by objects results in shadows. They investigate how shadows change over time. Students will:

- recognise that light appears to travel in straight lines
- remember that we see light sources because light from the source enters our eyes
- explore how light can be reflected from surfaces
- find out about how mirrors work and why they are very useful to us
- build on ideas about how light forms shadows to understand their shape and size
- investigate how shadows from the Sun change over time
- discover how light is measured.

> ### Key words
>
> beam, light intensity, light source, mirror, opaque, ray, reflect, shadow, silhouette, translucent, transparent

Scientific enquiry skills

This unit helps students to develop and practise the following scientific enquiry skills.

Scientific enquiry skill	Page
Plan and/or carry out enquiries to answer questions	70–71, 73–74, 76, 79, 81–83, 85, 87–89, 90–93, 95–96, 98–99
Make predictions	74, 79, 87–88, 91, 99
Recognise and control variables	74, 83, 85, 92, 95, 98–99
Make observations	70–76, 78–79, 81–85, 87–89, 92–93, 95–99
Take measurements, using equipment accurately	70–71, 83, 92–93, 96–99
Record data and results	70, 74, 76, 79, 82–83, 85, 87–89, 91–93, 95–99
Analyse data, notice patterns and group or classify things	70, 74, 76, 81–83, 85, 87–89, 92–93, 95–100
Report and present findings	70–71, 73–74, 76, 78–80, 83, 85, 88–89, 91–93, 95–100
Draw conclusions and give explanations	70–74, 76, 79, 83–85, 87–89, 92–93, 95, 97–100
Identify causal relationships	70, 74, 83, 85, 88–89, 92–93, 98–100

Ways to help

- Encourage students to review their prior work by asking them to explain what they already know about shadows.
- Ask students to regularly observe shadows and point out any changes during the day.
- Display photographs of shadows in the same place but at different times of the day.
- Arrange for a very dark part of the room or school to be available to demonstrate the lack of light.
- Encourage students to explore mirrors to see how light reflects.
- Obtain or make simple ray boxes to show narrow beams or rays of light.

Helping with activities

The following guidance gives you advice on how to help students with each activity.

Is there a link between sight and taste?

Explain that by seeing food your brain is already preparing to deal with messages from the taste buds.

How important is sight?

Point out that tapping and echoes from a room can give us a clue about our surroundings, even if we cannot see them.

Tricking your eyes
Give students access to the internet to find examples of optical illusions, or you could print off a number of examples and arrange these around the room.

Making a science animated film
Encourage students to research their science idea and then recommend they split it up into 20 or more stages to make the animation move smoothly.

Shining back
Spread varied objects around the room and ensure that some are dark and dull (such as black cloth) and others are bright and shiny (such as chrome ornaments).

Artificial light
Explain that the word 'artificial' means it has been made by a person or people – or by a machine made by people. It comes from the Latin word for handicraft (*artificis*).

The mirrored image
Point out that, although the image in a plane (flat) mirror is reversed (left becomes right and right becomes left), it is not inverted. Top does not become bottom.

Mirror writing
Allow students to make up their own messages to send to each other. This models one of the earliest codes.

Making a periscope
Make sure students have the mirrors set at exactly 45° otherwise the light from the object will not reach their eye and they will not see it.

Guiding light
Students could try to work out the problem using trial and error. However, ask them to think back to their work with the periscope to give them a clue how to progress.

Mirrors and design
Ask students to discuss where they have seen mirrors and what they were used for. List any they mention in three columns: mainly decorative; used to cast light; used to make a room appear larger.

Make a pinhole camera
Explain that the image seen on the screen of the pinhole camera is inverted (upside down). This is because light from the bottom of the object, for example, travels in a straight line. Therefore, after the light passes through the hole it continues and must hit the top of the screen.

Having fun with mirrors
Help students to remember the difference between convex and concave mirrors. Tell them that caves go inwards and so do concave mirrors.

Does light travel in straight lines?
Explain that if light could bend around corners, it would pass through the holes even if the cards were not lined up. This doesn't happen, so light must travel in straight lines.

Investigating refraction
Explain that refraction can make objects underwater appear much closer. Show students photographs of different examples of refraction in water.

Colour investigation
Provide a range of filters, or even transparent sweet wrappers, so students can explore a wide range of different colours.

Does it let light through or block light?
Explain to students that they will need to use the words more than once to fill in the gaps.

Translucent, transparent and opaque objects
Have large word cards in your room so that students become familiar with these key terms.

Does it make a good shadow?
Remind students that in order to make a clear shadow the light has to be blocked. This should give them a huge clue about opaque materials.

Investigating translucent and opaque materials
Allow students to use their imaginations to design different ways to test how much light passes through the materials. They could use a light meter, or they could judge the darkness of shadows against a spectrum of very light grey to black squares.

Making shadows
Encourage students to not only make the shapes suggested, but also to vary the size of the shapes by moving their hands towards or away from the light source.

Making silhouettes
Ask students to investigate the distance between the light source and the person, and the person and the screen to get a sharp and not a blurred image.

Investigate the size of shadows
Remind students to carry out measurements more than once and calculate an average to reduce error.

Moving shadow puppets
Help students to see the relationship between the light source movement and the shadow movement by explaining they will always be in the opposite direction.

Shadow hide and seek
Select a suitable place for the game so that there are objects such as trees to hide behind, but the area is not so dense with objects that the Sun cannot create shadows.

Does the darkness of shadows change during the day?
Explain to students that many things can change how dark a shadow looks. These include reflected light from objects, artificial light from windows and how opaque the object casting the shadow is.

Make a sundial

Stress that students should not move the sundial between measurements or that will invalidate their results.

Telling the time with shadows

Explain that it is an important part of any design process to test a prototype, evaluate it and then work on improvements.

Measuring light intensity

Point out that a tiny piece of tissue will block some light from hitting the solar strip, but that, if the light is bright, it will still allow the calculator to work. They can experiment with different layers of tissue until the calculator stops working.

Which light source will be brightest?

Point out that in order to make this a fair test each piece of the tissue paper should be the same thickness.

Light intensity timeline

Explain that a timeline sets out activities, events or inventions along a line that shows when they happened and in what order.

Distance and light intensity

Remind students that scientists will place the variable they are deciding on (the independent variable) along the X-axis. In this case, that is the distance from the source. The dependent variable goes along the Y-axis. In this case, that is the light intensity.

4 Building Electrical Circuits

What students will learn

This unit helps students to understand more about electricity and how to build and test electrical circuits. They explore conductors and insulators and assemble circuits from different components. Students investigate the effects of changing the number and voltage of cells (batteries). They predict and test what happens when components in a circuit are changed and represent circuits by using circuit diagrams. Students will:

- find out how some materials are better conductors and insulators of electricity than others
- find out how some metals are good conductors of electricity and most other materials are not
- understand why metals are used for cables and wires and why plastics are used to cover wires and as covers for plugs and switches
- learn how changing the number and voltage of cells affects the components in a circuit
- predict and test the effects of making changes to circuits
- draw diagrams of series circuits using standard symbols.

Scientific enquiry skills

This unit helps students to develop and practise the following scientific enquiry skills.

Scientific enquiry skill	Page
Plan and/or carry out enquiries to answer questions	105, 107, 109, 112–113, 115, 117, 118–120, 123, 125
Make predictions	107, 112–113, 119, 123, 125
Recognise and control variables	107, 112–113, 125
Make observations	105, 107, 109, 113, 115–116, 118–121, 123, 125
Take measurements, using equipment accurately	107, 109, 113, 120
Record data and results	105, 107, 109, 112–113, 115, 118–120, 123
Analyse data, notice patterns and group or classify things	105, 107, 109, 113, 115–116, 118–120
Report and present findings	105–107, 109, 112–113, 115, 118–120, 125
Draw conclusions and give explanations	105, 107, 109, 112–113, 115–116, 118–120, 123, 125
Identify causal relationships	107, 109, 112–113, 118–120

Ways to help

- Encourage students to learn the symbols of the components by displaying them around the room.
- Arrange incomplete circuits so students can fault find and repair the circuits.
- Ask students to think about why it is important to have both conducting and insulating materials.
- Encourage students to use circuit diagrams whenever they represent/draw a circuit.

Helping with activities

The following guidance gives you advice on how to help students with each activity.

Explain conductors and insulators

Display some devices and appliances that have parts that conduct (e.g. wires and parts of the plugs) and parts that insulate (e.g. the plastic coating on wires).

Is it an insulator?

Demonstrate how to set up the test circuit and show how the two unconnected wires can have crocodile clips on to allow other materials to be placed across the gap.

Research project: Ampère

Arrange for students to have access to the internet if possible. If not, you could download and print information about Ampère.

Investigate the conductivity of metals

Provide a range of metals such as pieces of copper wire or pipe, steel and aluminium strips cut from cans and zinc rings.

Wiring a plug

Explain that across the world there can be different designs for plugs and even different colours for the wires. Show some examples.

What have you learned so far?

Encourage students to attempt the questions to review their learning and then allow them to look back to research what they could not answer.

Changing the components in a circuit

Explain to students that they can change the number of batteries or bulbs in a circuit or add or remove other components, but only one at a time. Their circuit will always need to include at least one bulb.

Investigating the thickness of a wire

Point out that the thickness of a wire can be imagined like a door. A wide door will let more people pass through at the same time than a narrow door. A thick wire will let more electricity pass through at the same time than a narrow wire.

How does a filament bulb work?

Hand round or display some examples of filament bulbs. You can show large room light versions and small torch versions. Many bulbs are being replaced with LEDs, but you should be able to find some filament ones.

Does the width of a wire affect how hot it gets?

Explain that a fuse is an example of a circuit breaker. It is the weakest part of a circuit and so will fail (or burn out) before more expensive parts. Fuse wire is placed in a fireproof container so it is safe.

Using circuit diagrams

Display the symbols for the components in your room so students become familiar with them. Encourage them to use circuit diagrams to represent the circuit they construct.

Drawing circuits

Remind students that they always need to link components with connecting wires. These wires are always drawn as straight lines with 90° corners in a circuit.

Build circuits from diagrams and test them

Encourage a logical, step-by-step approach to fault finding. Students should start at the battery and check if it is connected and is the correct way round. They then follow the circuit clockwise – testing each connection then each component.

Investigating series and parallel circuits

Set up a series and a parallel circuit to show students the difference. Explain that the parallel circuit gives the flow/current of electricity two possible paths.

Using a voltmeter

Demonstrate how the voltmeter is not connected in series (in a line) as an ammeter is. Instead, it is set up in parallel. This means the meter is measuring the difference before and after a component.

Making a battery

Explain that the metal coins react with the lemon juice to create negatively charged particles called electrons. These are pushed around the circuit as an electrical current.

Model circuits

For greatest effect, and to make the task and content more memorable, provide the largest possible paper plates or card so the circuit models are huge. Display them around the room so they look spectacular.

Circuit wordsearch

Suggest that students look in the puzzle for the first letter of the first word in the list and then search around that for the second letter, and so on.

5 Adaptation and Inherited Characteristics

What students will learn

This unit helps students to understand more about how living things are adapted to their habitats and how characteristics are passed from parents to their offspring. Students study examples of how living things have changed over time and link this to the ways that animals and plants have to be adapted to their habitat to survive. They review that living things do not live forever and so must have offspring to ensure the survival of the species. Students study how offspring vary from their parents and that this can eventually lead to new species. Students will:

- recognise that living things have changed over time
- learn that fossils give us information about living things that lived on Earth millions of years ago
- review that living things produce offspring
- recognise that offspring vary and are not identical to their parents

- identify how animals and plants are adapted to suit their environment in different ways
- learn that adaptation may lead to new species.

> ### Key words
> adaptation, ancestor, characteristic, environment, extinct, fossil, habitat, inherit, offspring, reproduction, species, variation

Scientific enquiry skills

This unit helps students to develop and practise the following scientific enquiry skills.

Scientific enquiry skill	Page
Plan and/or carry out enquiries to answer questions	132, 134–135, 137–138, 141
Make predictions	132, 135, 141
Recognise and control variables	132, 135, 141
Make observations	127–128, 130–138, 141
Take measurements, using equipment accurately	129, 132, 134–135, 141
Record data and results	132, 134–135, 138, 141
Analyse data, notice patterns and group or classify things	128, 130, 132, 134–135, 138–139, 141
Report and present findings	127, 129, 132, 134–135, 137–138, 141
Draw conclusions and give explanations	128, 130–132, 134–136, 138–139, 141
Identify causal relationships	130, 132, 135, 136–139, 141

Ways to help

- Display pictures of a range of different living things and their offspring.
- Review prior knowledge by asking students questions about how different living things are adapted to their habitats.
- Display examples of fossils to show life that existed on Earth a long time ago.
- Encourage students to identify how offspring that look very similar to their parents do vary slightly.

Helping with activities

The following guidance gives you advice on how to help students with each activity.

How are fossils formed?
Allow students to work individually for a few minutes first. Then come together as a class to discuss their answers. Work through the hint together if students need more support.

Making a plaster cast fossil model
Explain that some fossils are the remains of a living thing but most are made when substances fill moulds of the living thing.

Handling data about change
Remind students to find the correct era (period of time) for each animal and then label this on the X-axis (horizontal) so each horse ancestor has its own bar.

Changes in plants
Stress that farmers have been selecting desired characteristics in plants for thousands of years.

Seed investigation
Explain that there is no direct link between the size and appearance of a seed and the plant that made them, but the offspring (young plants) will grow to look very similar to the parent plants.

Find the parent
Encourage students to think back and discuss their earlier work on the life cycle of animals, and especially animals that have offspring that do not look like the adult – such as frogs and butterflies.

Investigating variation in hand size
Explain that with natural variation there are usually a few people with hand sizes that are very large or very small, but most will cluster around a central value. This gives what is often called a bell or normal distribution curve – it is bell shaped.

Investigating variation in plants
Remind students to only alter one variable (the independent variable). This is the type of seeds in this case. The dependent variable is what they are measuring – the height of the plants.

Adaptations for feeding
Encourage students to use their observation skills to note the details of the beaks of each bird and then link this to how each beak is best adapted for certain foods.

Plant adaptation survey
Point out that, although plants do not move around and may not seem as alive as animals, they also need to be well adapted to survive in their habitat.

Adaptation trail
Set students a challenge to hide the model insects as well as they can to make it difficult for people to find them. This will reinforce ideas of camouflage and adaptation to reduce predation.

Capture release data
Explain that predators will find prey animals that are not well adapted to a habitat and eat more of these. These prey animals will be less likely to be recaptured.

Key words

1 Find some of the key words for this unit hidden in the wordsearch.

Circle each word when you find it in the grid below. One example has been done for you.

> acid rain conservation deforestation environment
> habitat ~~landfill~~ litter pollution recycle

l	l	i	f	d	n	a	l	l	e	i	e	i	r
a	d	e	f	o	r	e	s	t	a	t	i	o	n
l	i	i	o	r	t	a	c	i	d	r	a	i	n
o	e	e	r	l	i	e	e	c	t	i	l	e	n
c	o	n	s	e	r	v	a	t	i	o	n	f	v
n	d	h	p	o	l	l	u	t	i	o	n	t	i
v	u	i	i	a	n	n	h	a	b	i	t	a	t
r	e	i	n	n	o	t	r	u	a	p	t	t	o
i	f	y	l	b	a	a	d	l	o	e	t	a	a
e	n	v	i	r	o	n	m	e	n	t	r	e	m
o	r	c	l	a	u	n	l	l	r	c	f	d
i	c	t	a	i	l	i	t	t	e	r	l	m	a
k	e	y	v	e	n	t	n	t	n	e	t	e	a
f	d	r	e	c	y	c	l	e	l	i	a	a	y

2 There is one word in the wordsearch that is not listed in the box. The word begins with 'k'.

Circle the word in the grid and write the word here. _____

3 Write a definition of this word. You have studied it before.

Introduction

Test your key word memory!

 1 Look at the key words on page 14 of your Student Book for 30 seconds.

Close the book and try the activity below.

2 Write in the missing letters for the key words.

e ____ ____ ____ r ____ ____ m ____ ____ t

____ p e ____ ____ e ____

c ____ ____ ____ e r ____ ____ t ____ ____ n

p ____ ____ ____ u ____ ____ ____ n

k ____ ____

____ i ____ g d ____ ____

g ____ ____ ____ n ____ ____ ____ s e e ____ ____ ____ c ____

____ ____ f ____ r ____ s ____ ____ t ____ ____ n

If you need to, you can look back at your Student Book for another 30 seconds.

3 Ask a partner to check your words. Check theirs.

Identifying the correct kingdom

staphylococcus   amoeba   Euglena   spirillum

mushroom   mould   fern   hibiscus   seaweed

fish   crab   worm   camel

Some examples from each of the main groups of living things are shown above.

1 Which kingdoms do these living things belong to? Use the information in your Student Book to help you to classify each one into its correct kingdom.

2 Record your answers in the table below. One answer has been done for you.

Kingdom	Examples
prokaryotes (bacteria and some algae)	
protists (organisms made up of one cell)	
fungi (moulds, toadstools)	mushrooms
plants	
animals	

3 Which of the animals are vertebrates?

4 Which one of the plants is a flowering plant?

The Prokaryote kingdom is also known as the kingdom Monera.

Plant classification survey

This activity supports the investigation on page 17 of your Student Book.

1 Look at the plant classification key on page 17 of your Student Book.

Ferns

Conifers

Sunflowers

Algae

Mosses

2 Go out into your local area to look for different plants.

If possible, look at some pond water through a hand lens or microscope. This will help you to find small plants such as green algae.

3 Draw or take photographs of any plants you observe.

4 Find some plants from each major group in your area. Use the diagram in your Student Book to help you.

Warning! Stay with your group. Do not touch any plants without permission from an adult. Discuss why this is important.

5 Record the types of plants you find in the table below.

Type of plant	Examples observed (e.g. green algae, red algae)	Location – where you found this plant
algae		
mosses		
ferns		
conifers		
flowering plants		

6 Present your findings as an information leaflet.

Using characteristics to classify animals

Classifying animals

 This activity supports the investigation on page 18 of your Student Book.

1 Choose four animals from the list:

- lion or lioness
- snowshoe hare
- frog
- butterfly
- snake
- eagle

2 Use the table below to help you classify these animals. One example has been added to help you.

Animal	Characteristics	How does this help the animal to survive?	Which group or class of animals does the animal belong to?
grouper	• body covered in scales • fins • gills	• makes the animal smooth to pass through water • helps the animal move • allows the animal to breathe underwater	vertebrates – fish

Stretch zone

One of the animals in the list is not a vertebrate.

a Name this animal.

_____

b Why is it not classed as a vertebrate?

_____

Different shaped beaks

This activity supports the investigation on page 19 of your Student Book.

1 Try to pick up each of the different seeds. Use the different tools you have been given.

2 Use the table below to record the results from your investigation.

Diagram/description of forceps used	Seed diagram and measurement	Number of seeds picked up

3 Did the shape of the forceps change the number of seeds you could pick up?

4 Circle the appropriate answer:

These results **support / contradict** the idea that the shape of the beak makes it easier to pick up some seeds more than others.

Stretch zone

Research the following birds: eagle, parrot, spoonbill, hummingbird.

Plan a short report to tell people how the birds' beaks are adapted to the food they eat.

Using characteristics to classify plants and microorganisms

Classifying local plants

 This activity supports the investigation on page 20 of your Student Book.

Survey the plants in your local area.

1 Complete the table below to record your observations.

Warning! Some plants can be toxic or cause irritation. Do not touch any plants. Always wash your hands after investigations.

Diagram/description of the plant's characteristics	How can these help the plant to survive?	Name of plant

2 a Put the plants you have found into different groups:

b How many groups did you make?

_____

3 Could some plants be in more than one of your groups? Explain how.

Researching microorganisms

1   Read the following statements:

> **A** Scientists used to classify these as plants. They often grow in fresh or salt water or underground in damp places. They have chlorophyll but no stems, roots or leaves.

> **B** These are a large group of one-celled organisms. They can live in water or as parasites. They use their cilia or flagella to move about.

> **C** These are definitely living things. They are not the biggest or the smallest type. They can cause some infections like food poisoning.

> **D** Some of these microorganisms are made of many cells, but others only one. They can be very large. They are the biggest microorganism. These can be used in baking.

> **E** The largest microorganism is approximately 0.0000003 mm big. Some scientists do not classify them as microorganisms as they cannot live outside other cells. They are often linked to pandemics.

2   Research each of the following microorganisms:

- algae
- bacteria
- fungi
- protozoa
- viruses

3   Link each statement in question 1 to the correct type of microorganism listed in question 2.

A: _____   D: _____

B: _____   E: _____

C: _____

4   Name one example of each type of microorganism.

A: _____   D: _____

B: _____   E: _____

C: _____

Making your own classification key

You are going to classify a selection of birds.

Here is an example of a classification key.

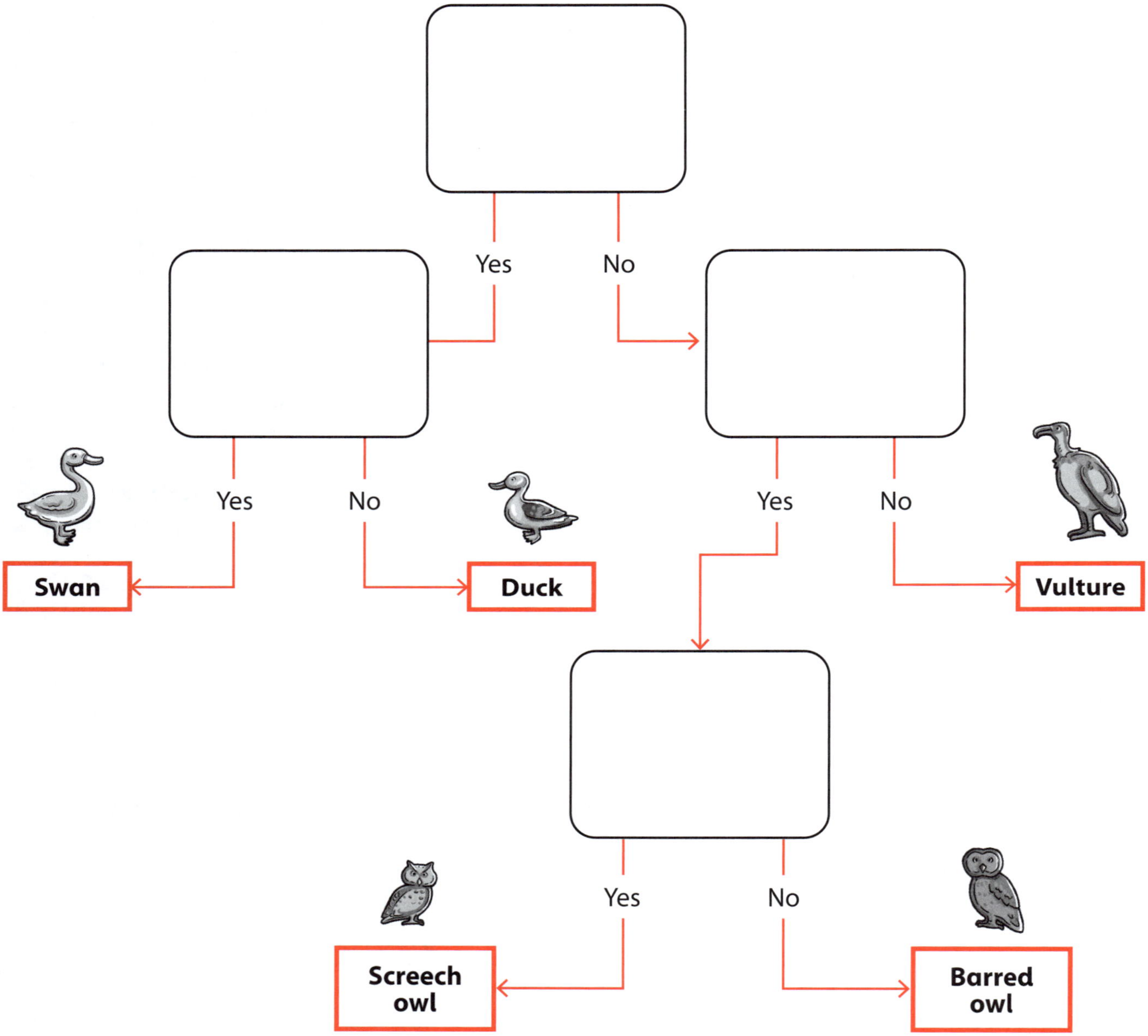

Yes   No

Yes   No

Yes   No

Swan

Duck

Vulture

Yes   No

Screech owl

Barred owl

1. Look at the key. The questions are missing.

2. You need to help someone identify the birds. Discuss the questions that you could ask at each stage. Write your questions in the boxes.

3. Test your questions with other students. Which questions work best? Which need to be improved?

Designing a classification key

This activity supports the investigation on page 23 of your Student Book.

1 Write down the name of the living thing you are going to classify and identify.

_____

2 List the characteristics of this living thing. Try to think of four or five.

The characteristics must be things that do not change very much over time.

A good choice is the number of legs, or if an animal has scales. A poor choice would be whether a plant has leaves (as the leaves may be there for part of the year and lost at other times), or the size of a plant or animal.

Record these characteristics in the left-hand column of the table below.

Characteristics of the living thing	A 'yes' or 'no' question I can use in my key

3 Why is size not a very good characteristic to use in a classification key?

4 Write down a 'yes' or 'no' question to ask about each characteristic. Add these to the right-hand column of the table. Examples of 'yes' or 'no' questions are:

- Does the animal have eight legs?
- Does the animal have a hard shell?

Do not use open questions such as: What colour is the animal?

5 Draw your key on a large sheet of paper.

6 Test your key on other students. How well did it work?

7 Think of one improvement you would make to your key.

Looking after our world

Protecting our environment

1 Use the words in the box to help you complete the sentences below.

> activities endangered extinct forests habitat
> living medicines natural plants protect

There are many animals and plants that are _____. We will lose

these species forever if we don't _____ them and their

_____ habitats. They will become _____.

(A species is a type of _____ thing.)

A _____ is where an animal or plant lives. Many animals and

plants are lost because of human _____. Hunting and cutting down

_____ can destroy natural habitats and the animals and

_____ that live there.

There are many plants that we have not discovered yet. They may help us

with _____ or other useful things.

2 Why are some animals endangered? _____

_____

3 How can we protect endangered species? _____

_____

4 Write down two human activities that destroy natural habitats.

- _____

- _____

Conservation project

 Discuss conservation projects around the world. Why do we need conservation projects?

 Research a conservation project in your area.

1 Find out about conservation projects in the local area.

    a Ask people if they know about any local conservation projects.

    b Use the internet or local newspapers to find out more.

2 Choose one project. Find out as much as you can about the project.

3 Make an information leaflet or booklet about this project.

    a Make sure your leaflet answers some of these questions:

- What are the main aims of the conservation project?
- Which living things does the project aim to protect?
- What is it protecting the living things from?
- How will the project protect the living things?
- When did the project start? If it hasn't already started, when does it plan to start?
- How long will it take to complete the project?
- What will happen after the project is complete?
- Who is giving money for the project?
- Will there be any events to raise money for the project?
- How can local people help with the project?

    b On your leaflet, draw a picture of some of the living things protected by this project.

Air pollution

Investigate the greenhouse effect

You will need: pieces of dowelling or some skewers, some clear plastic bags or plastic food wrap, a thermometer.

 Make a model of the greenhouse effect.

1 Make a polythene greenhouse.

- Use pieces of dowelling or skewers to construct a frame.
- Cover the frame in clear plastic bags or plastic food wrap.

2 Decide where to place your greenhouse.

- It will need to be in the Sun.
- It must not be moved or changed during the investigation.

3 Predict whether the temperature will be higher inside or outside your greenhouse.

4 Use a thermometer to take the temperature inside and outside the greenhouse.

5 Record the temperature at different times of day for two days.

Day 1 Time	Temp. inside greenhouse (°C)	Temp. outside greenhouse (°C)	Day 2 Time	Temp. inside greenhouse (°C)	Temp. outside greenhouse (°C)

6 Can you see a pattern in your results?

a As the temperature increased outside, did it increase in the greenhouse?   **yes   no**

b Was the temperature higher or lower inside the greenhouse than outside? _____

c What does this tell us about the greenhouse effect on Earth? _____

_____

d How is the greenhouse effect affecting the temperature on Earth? _____

_____

The greenhouse effect

```
atmosphere      atmosphere traps greenhouse gases
        Earth heats up      Sun's rays
```

 1 Label the diagram. Use the words in the box.

2 List two gases that help to cause the greenhouse effect.

3 Explain how the greenhouse effect can damage habitats and lead to problems for animals and plants.

4 Describe two ways in which the greenhouse effect could be reduced.

Stone survey

Stone cut from rocks in the ground has been used for thousands of years.

1 Survey your local area to find out how stone is being used. Stone may be used as large building blocks or as smaller pebbles for roads.

2 Record different examples in the table.

Type of rock	What it is being used for

3 Complete the sentence:

Rocks are very important because they _____

_____ .

Deforestation debate

Imagine you are going to join the debate: should we stop cutting down trees? A debate is where people take it in turns to present their arguments about an issue. They try to persuade other people that their ideas are correct.

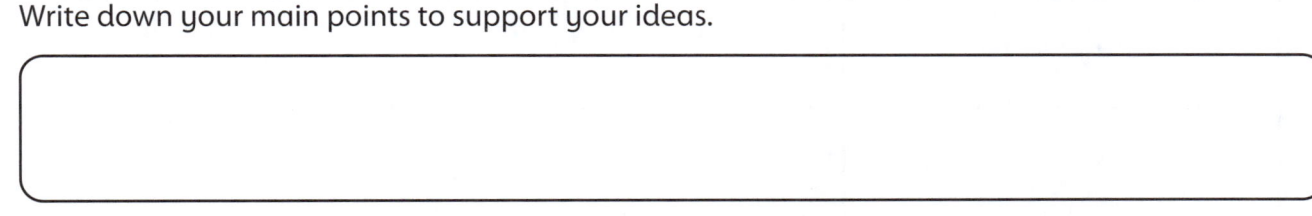

We need to cut down trees to give us fuel for fires. We also wouldn't have paper or spaces to build houses and farms. What would life be like without wood for furniture or buildings?

If we cut down trees, then plants and animals will die. Soil will be washed away and burning wood adds to the greenhouse effect. We can use alternative materials instead of wood.

You will be asked to take the side of one of the people opposite.

1   Find out more about each of their arguments and possible arguments against it.

2   Plan how you would speak in favour of your argument and be ready to question the other side.

3   Write down your main points to support your ideas.

4   Predict what the other side might say. Think of some arguments against their ideas.

5   Carry out the debate. At the end of the debate, vote for or against the statement:

Cutting down trees should be stopped.

6   What was the result of the vote?

For = _____

Against = _____

How cloudy is the water?

Polluted water often has particles of dirt floating in it. This makes the water cloudy or turbid. How turbid or how clear water is can show how polluted it is.

 You are going to measure the turbidity of water. You will be given five water samples to test.

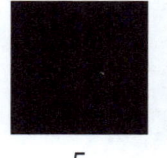    

| 5 | 4 | 3 | 2 | 1 |

1 Place each water sample over the squares above. Look down through the water sample.

2 Which numbered square can you see? Record the number in the table below.

Sample number	Number of square visible	Most or least turbid?

3 Decide which is the most turbid or cloudy sample and which is the least turbid.

4 Why is turbidity (cloudiness) not a completely reliable measure of water pollution?

Waste disposal in the local area

1 Talk to other people about waste.

- What is waste?
- What do you put in your dustbin?
- Could anything you put there be recycled or reused?
- Where does your waste go?

2 a Research waste disposal in your local area. Use the internet or interview local people you know to find out as much as you can about waste disposal.

b Plan a short report about the information you find.

Make sure your report answers these questions:

- How is the waste collected?
- Where does the waste go?
- Is any of the waste recycled?

3 Make a poster that encourages people to think about reducing waste and recycling.

- Copy this symbol onto a piece of paper or card.

- Write some information to persuade people to reduce the amount of waste they produce.
- Encourage people to recycle or reuse waste items.

4 Your teacher will tell you where to display your poster so that it will make people think about waste disposal.

Saving energy at home

Look at the picture.

1 Talk about these questions:

- Which of the devices in the picture use energy?
- What do the devices do?
- Which devices have you got in your house?

2 Choose and find out about one electrical device that is used a lot. Draw a table to record:

- how often people use the device
- how long they use it for.

3 Place your table next to the device for one week. Ask people to record every time they use the device and how long they use it for.

4 At the end of the week, use the table to calculate the total amount of time the device is used each week.

The _____ in my home is used for _____ hours

and _____ minutes per week.

5 Use the internet to find out the energy consumption of the device. This is the amount of energy the device uses per hour.

The _____ uses _____ of energy per hour.

6 Calculate how much energy is being used by the device in your home in:

a a day: _____

b a week: _____

c a year: _____

School energy survey

This activity supports the investigation on page 33 of your Student Book.
You are going to survey your school to record the different uses of electricity.

1 Predict where you think the highest use of energy will be found.

2 List the devices you found and how each device could be used less.

Location in the school	Name of device	How the device could be used less

3 Plan an energy-saving leaflet for your school. Use the checklist to help you:

- description of each device
- picture of examples of devices
- explanation of how each device is used
- description of how each device could be used less
- explanation of how this would help reduce energy use and pollution

Recycling and reusing materials

Make a useful object from waste materials

You are going to look at a variety of waste materials.

1   Look at the materials and think about how you can reuse them.

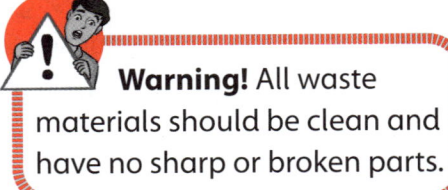

Warning! All waste materials should be clean and have no sharp or broken parts.

You could make a pencil holder or any other object. Try to think of a good use for the waste materials.

These students are making a mobile from coloured plastic bottles

2   Design your object in the boxes. List all the materials you will need. Remember to include materials for sticking the object together.

Materials I will need	Drawing of my design

3   Make your object.

If you make the object again, is there anything that you will change or do differently? Write any changes that you will make.

Interpreting recycling data

1 Talk about the materials that are recycled in your area.

2 Look at the graph. It shows how many aluminium cans are recycled in some countries.

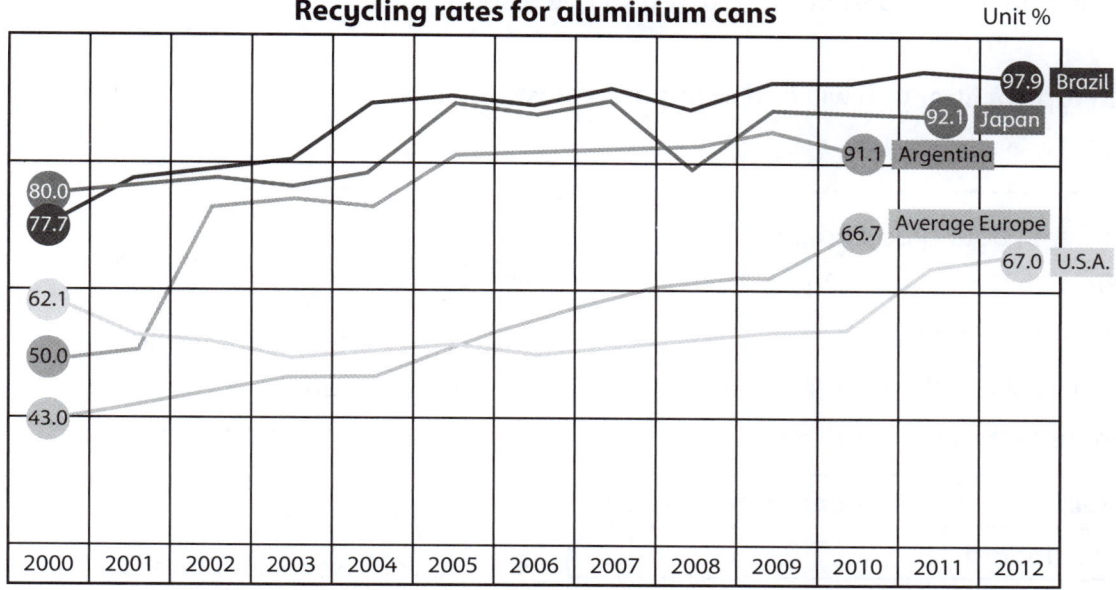

Recycling rates for aluminium cans — Unit %

Brazil 97.9, Japan 92.1, Argentina 91.1, Average Europe 66.7, U.S.A. 67.0

80.0, 77.7, 62.1, 50.0, 43.0

2000 2001 2002 2003 2004 2005 2006 2007 2008 2009 2010 2011 2012

Source: recyclingportal.eu

a Which country recycled the highest percentage of cans in 2012? _____

b Which country recycled the lowest percentage of cans in 2012? _____

c Which country recycled the highest percentage of cans in 2000? _____

d Which country has improved its recycling record the most since 2000? _____

e Describe the pattern of the data for the USA. _____

_____

f Describe the pattern of the data for Europe. _____

_____

g How can you help to increase the number of cans that are recycled in your country?

_____

Litter survey

This activity supports the investigation on page 36 of your Student Book.

You are going to carry out a survey of litter.

You will go outside and find an area to survey. You will be responsible for this area for one week.

1 Predict which type of litter you will find in this area most often.

_____

2 Collect any litter in your area and put it in a plastic bag.

3 Sort the litter into different types.

4 Count how many items of each type you find.

5 Record in the table the litter you find.

Warning!

- Check with an adult before you touch anything on the ground.
- Do not pick up anything sharp.
- Always wear gloves when you are collecting litter.
- Always wash your hands when you have finished collecting litter.

Type of litter	Number of items found
paper and cardboard	
metal	
plastic	
food waste	
glass	
wood	
polystyrene foam	
other	

6 Look at your table of results.

a Which type of litter is the most common? _____

b Why do you think this is? _____

_____

7 Imagine that an adult you know wants to encourage people to not drop litter. Discuss ways the person could do this. Here are some ideas:

- Talk to people and explain why they should not drop litter.
- Point out the litter bins and ask people to use them.
- Ask people to take their litter home if they cannot find a bin.
- Display information to remind people to keep the area free from litter.

Design an anti-litter poster

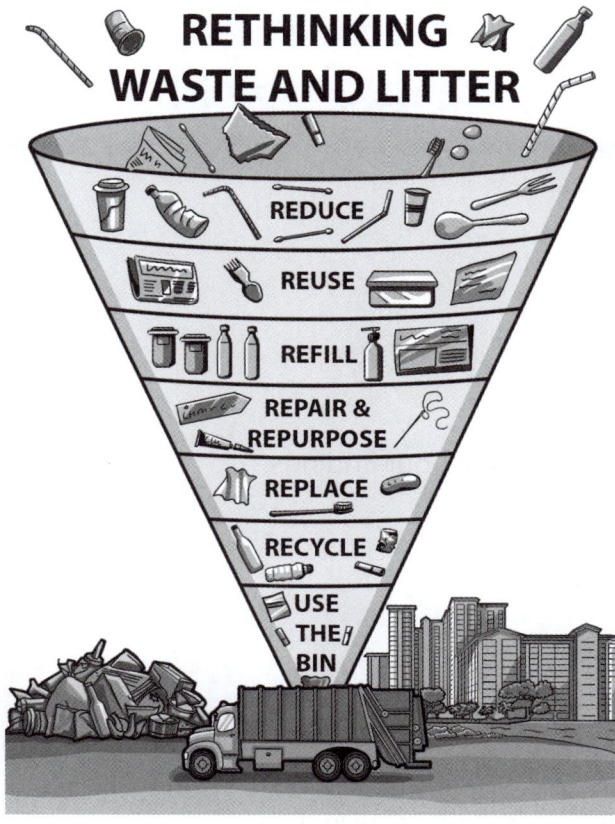

Posters can make people think about an issue.

They may have a lot of information or a simple message.

1 Design your own poster to encourage people to not drop litter.

Your poster will be displayed near litter bins in the school.

Make your poster:

- eye catching
- colourful
- informative.

2 Ask someone to look at your poster.

- Did it make them think?
- Have they changed their attitude to litter at all?

Protecting the environment

Air pollution

 Look around at all the appliances that use energy. Talk about how often these appliances are used.

1 Find out about how electricity is generated in your area.

- Which fuels are used to generate electricity?
- What pollution does this cause?
- What impact does this have on the environment?
- Does this affect the environment where you live?

2 Write a report or information leaflet or make a poster to display your findings.

3 How clean is the air in your local area?

You can test this by making a simple air filter.

> **You will need:** some white kitchen towel, tissue paper or a piece of clean fabric, sticky tape.

- Attach the kitchen towel, tissue or fabric to an open window. Use sticky tape to hold it in place. This is your air filter.
- The air will flow through the filter. If there is any air pollution, the filter will collect it.
- Check your filter throughout the day. If you can, leave it in place for more than one day.

4 Did your air filter collect any air pollution?   **yes**   **no**

5 Is the air that you breathe clean? Explain your answer. _____

_____

_____

Saving energy questionnaire

1 Use the questions below to carry out a survey of people at school or at home.

Question	Number of people who agree	Number of people who disagree
I do not waste energy.		
I use renewable energy a lot.		
There are factories near me that use a lot of energy.		
I save energy by always switching things off.		
I use energy-efficient devices all the time.		
I walk or take the bus rather than use a car.		
I avoid plastic packaging whenever possible.		
I always take my own bags when shopping.		
I never use single-use plastic bottles.		
I recycle as much as I can.		

2 Use the results of the survey to write a short newspaper report about how well energy is saved in your school and area.

What I have learned about classification and habitats

 What went well

1 Think about what you have learned.

2 Talk to a friend about something that went well in this unit.

3 Tick ✓ the boxes to rate yourself.

I can *describe* how living things are classified into broad groups.	That's easy. ⬜ That's challenging. ⬜	Pages 16–17
I can *use characteristics* to classify living things.	That's easy. ⬜ That's challenging. ⬜	Pages 18–21
I can *use classification Keys* to group living things.	That's easy. ⬜ That's challenging. ⬜	Pages 22–23
I Know that humans have positive and negative effects on the environment.	That's easy. ⬜ That's challenging. ⬜	Pages 24–31
I have explored a number of ways of caring for the environment.	That's easy. ⬜ That's challenging. ⬜	Pages 32–39

If you want to know more or need to check, go back to the pages in your Student Book.

Investigate like a scientist

Measuring surfaces as evidence of air pollution

You are going to use a method called surface wiping.

1 Use a piece of sticky tape that is 10 cm long to sample each surface. The tape will pick up any particles of pollution. Sample many surfaces using the surface wipe method. These could include:

- inside and outside walls
- floors
- trees
- posts and poles
- furniture
- windows
- doors.

2 You can also investigate if pollution varies with height.

Try measuring at different heights such as ground level, 0.5 metres, 1.0 metres and 1.5 metres.

3 Record your results in the table below. Give each strip a number:

- 1 for the cleanest strips
- 4 for the dirtiest strips

Location and surface	Height	Stick your tape here	Number 1–4

4 Write a project report to describe your method, your results and your conclusions about air pollution around your school.

2 Organs and Systems

Key words

m	d	m	e	v	k	r	z	f	o	f	l
s	e	b	q	h	c	a	m	o	t	n	i
g	f	d	v	n	k	c	b	r	a	r	f
n	b	c	i	p	p	o	s	g	j	u	e
u	d	v	i	c	z	c	r	a	f	k	s
l	m	c	n	k	i	o	k	n	u	s	t
p	a	l	e	k	t	n	t	e	n	x	y
e	d	v	n	z	c	i	e	j	c	e	l
y	v	c	e	p	o	r	p	j	t	n	e
u	v	a	c	c	i	n	e	x	i	c	q
v	l	z	b	j	n	x	d	m	o	v	v
d	r	u	g	n	x	u	b	t	n	r	o

> drug   function   lifestyle   medicine
> organ   vaccine

1 Circle some of the key words for this unit in the wordsearch.

2 Check the words on this page against the word cloud on page 43 of your Student Book. Write down any key words that are missing.

Introduction

Discussion notes

 1 Look at the photograph. Discuss the questions below.

2 Write some notes from your discussions. You can use bullet points to summarise your main ideas.

a Which parts of the body are the runners having to use to travel so quickly?

b Imagine the runners had not eaten anything for a few days, then they raced. Do you think they would run differently? How?

c Discuss why the runners have a higher heart rate immediately after the race than immediately before.

d What other changes might you notice about the runners after the race?

e Plan how you could test your idea about the runners and their heart rates before and after the run.

Where are our major organs?

Where are our organs?

Look at the outline of a human body. Test your knowledge of the organs.

1 Draw the organs listed in the box onto the outline. Try to draw each organ the correct size and in the correct place.

> brain   heart   intestines   kidneys
> liver   lungs   stomach

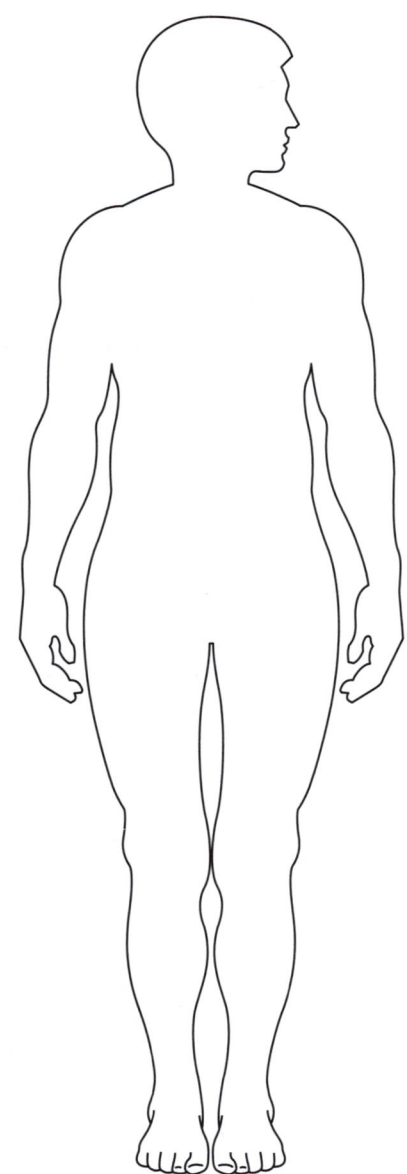

2 Ask someone else to label the organs you have drawn. Help them if they cannot name the organs.

Tracing the organs

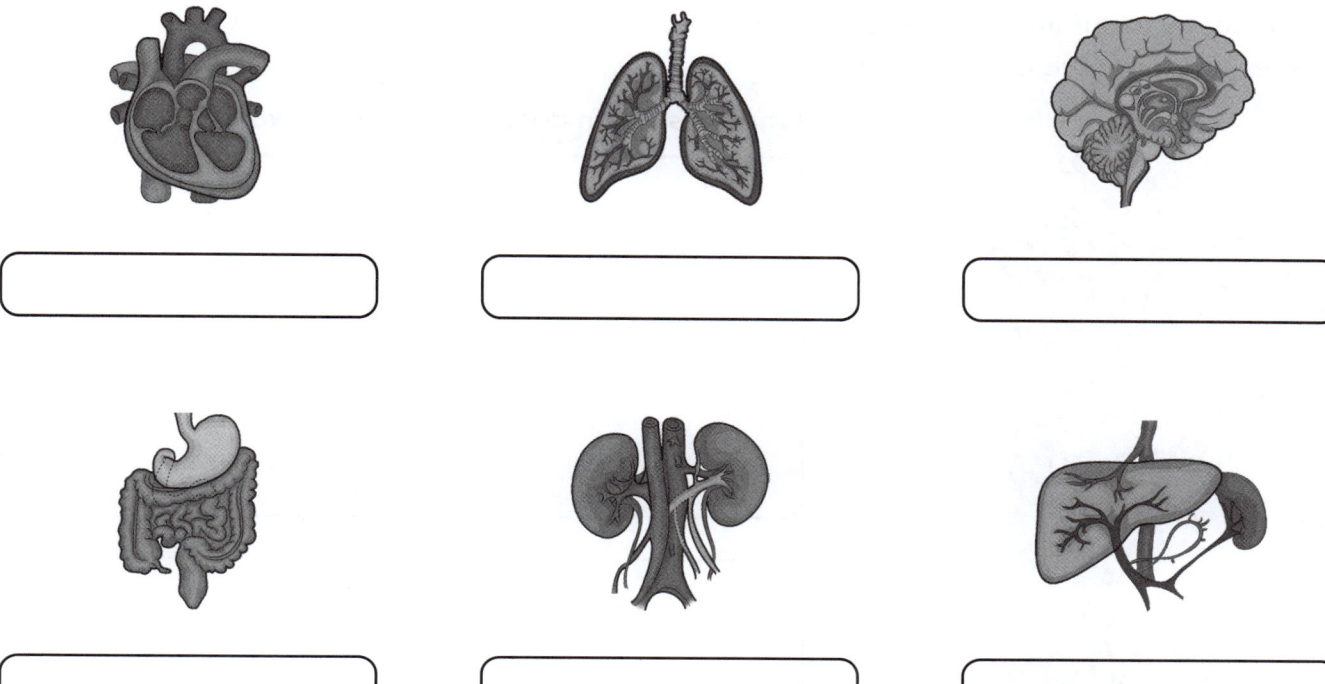

1   Look at the organs shown above. Write the name of each organ in the boxes.

2   Trace each organ onto a separate piece of paper:

   a   Place a piece of tracing paper over the diagram. Draw around the outline using a pencil.

   b   Place your tracing paper onto a clean sheet of paper.

   c   Draw over the traced lines again – pressing hard.

   d   When you lift the tracing paper, you will leave an imprint on the clean paper below.

   e   You can draw over your imprint to make it stand out. You can use a pen or a pencil for this.

3   Cut out your traced organs and use them to make a poster of a body. Take care to place the organs in the correct place on a body outline and label each one.

4   Colour in your poster and display it in the classroom.

Our heart, lungs and brain

1   Look at the diagrams of the organs. In the boxes, write what each organ does to
    keep you alive. This is its function.

What this organ does to keep you alive:

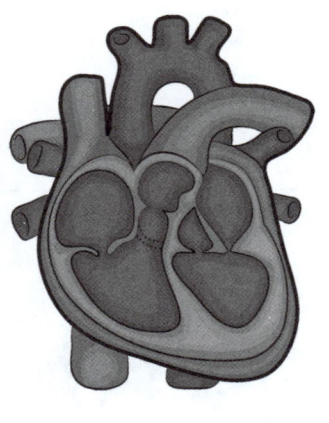

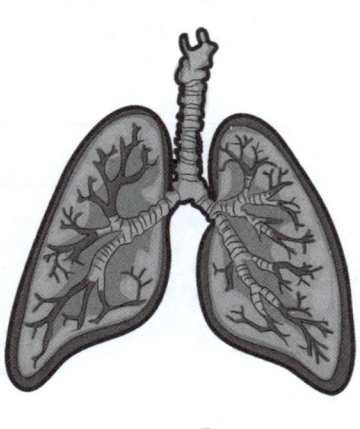

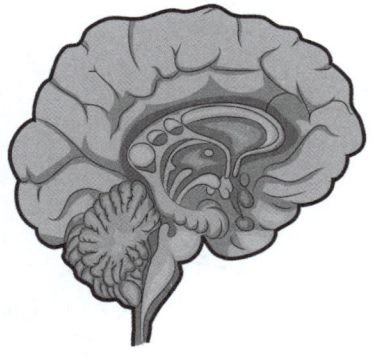

2   Which part of the skeleton protects the organ in the head?

_____

3   Which part of the skeleton protects the organs in the chest?

_____

Summary table

Major organ	What the organ does
	Acts as the body's control centre
	Break down food and take in water
	Pumps blood around the body
	Filter out ammonia and urea
	Take in air

brain   heart   kidneys   lungs   stomach and intestines

1 What does each organ do? Complete the table using words from the box.

2 Work with a partner. Take it in turns to read out the name of an organ from your table.

Point to where in your body that organ is found.

How we breathe

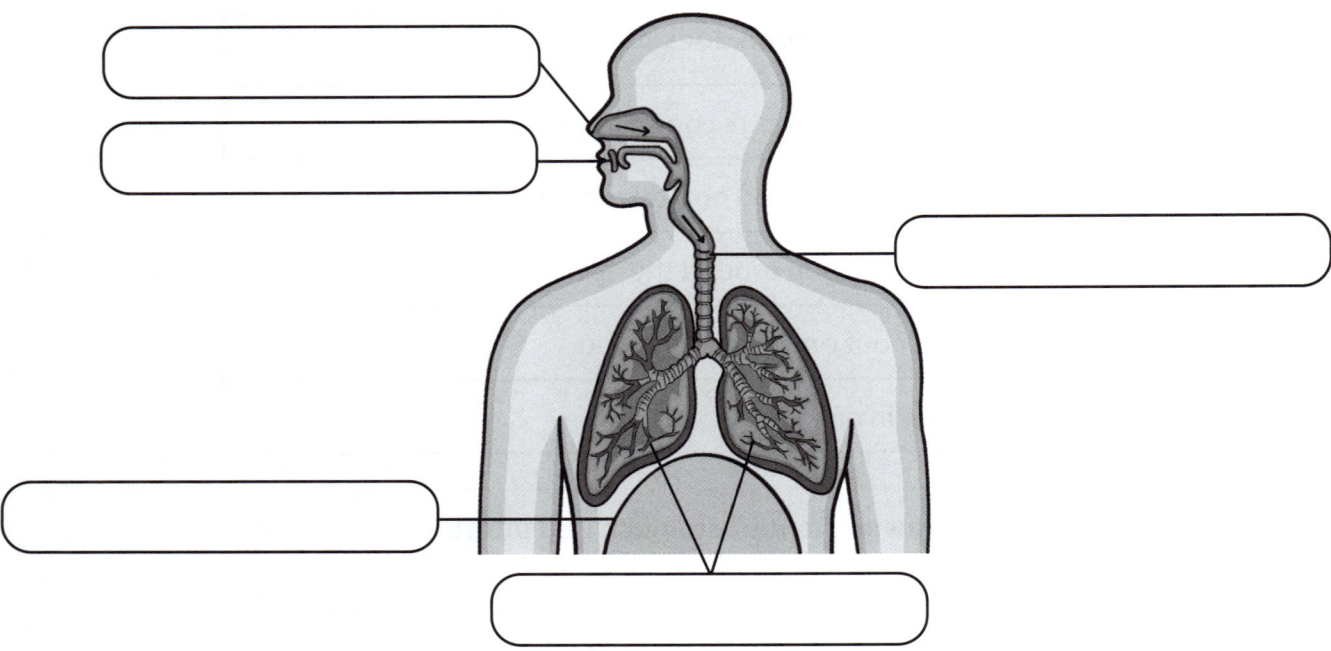

1   Label the diagram. Use words from the box.

diaphragm   lungs   mouth   nose   windpipe

2   Describe what happens to the ribs and diaphragm as a person breathes in.

3   Describe what happens to the ribs and diaphragm as a person breathes out.

Breathing rates

This activity supports the investigation on page 49 of your Student Book.

You are going to investigate breathing rates immediately before and immediately after exercise.

1 Write down the plan for your investigation.

2 How will you measure the differences between people?

3 How will you record your results?

4 List any safety rules you will follow.

5 Record your findings in the table.

Name of the person	Breathing rate immediately before exercise	Breathing rate immediately after exercise

6 Now design a presentation for the class. Tick ✓ which type of presentation you have decided to do:

- stand-up talk

- computer presentation

- poster

Label the parts of the circulatory system

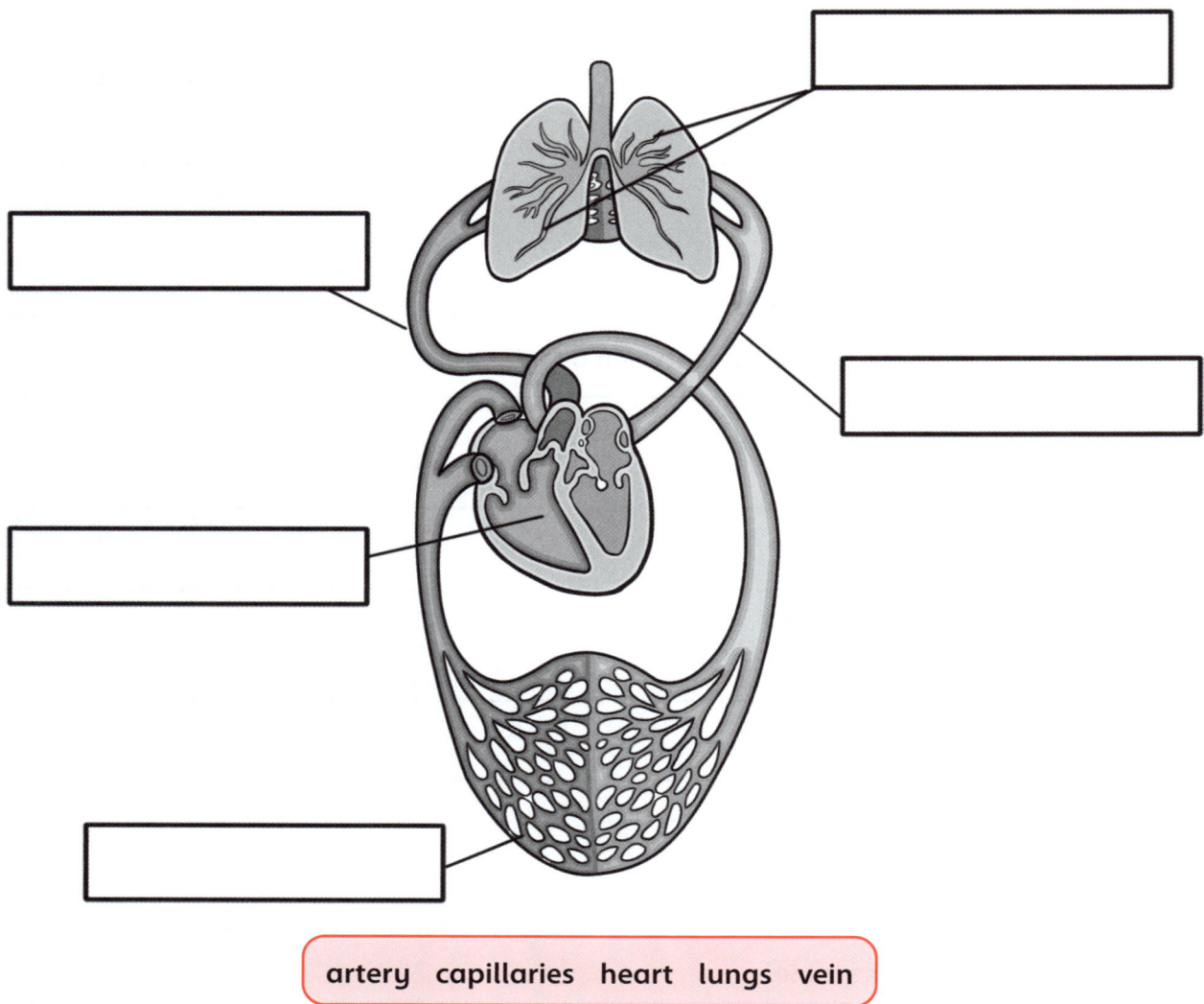

artery   capillaries   heart   lungs   vein

Label the diagram. Use words in the box.

Stretch zone

Explain why the artery that transports blood from the heart to the lungs is the only artery that transports blood that is not rich in oxygen.

Exercise, pulse rates and fitness

1 Which activities make our pulse rate increase the most? Draw a line from each activity to the correct pulse rate.

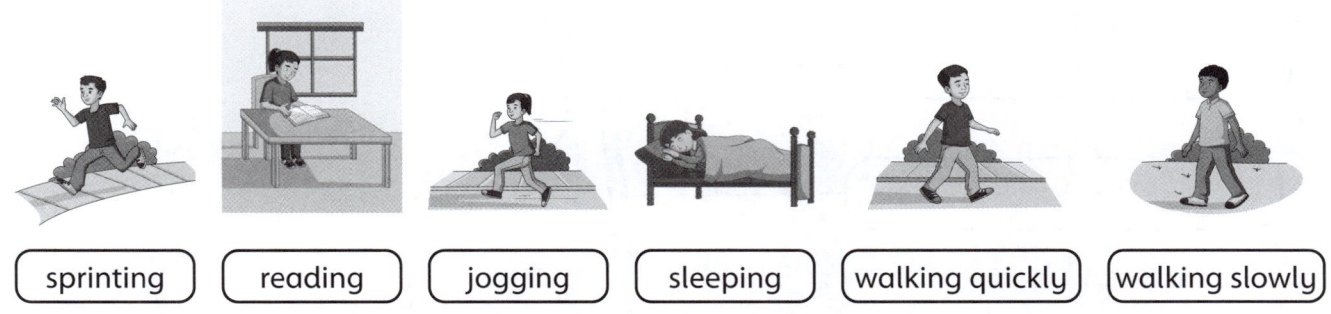

| sprinting | reading | jogging | sleeping | walking quickly | walking slowly |

| 67 bpm | 78 bpm | 95 bpm | 105 bpm | 120 bpm | 140 bpm |

Remember: bpm means beats per minute.

A very low pulse rate can indicate a good level of fitness. Some professional cyclists have a resting heart rate of less than 30 beats per minute!

2 When do you exercise most? _____

3 What happens to your pulse rate when you exercise? _____

The digestive system

Parts of the digestive system

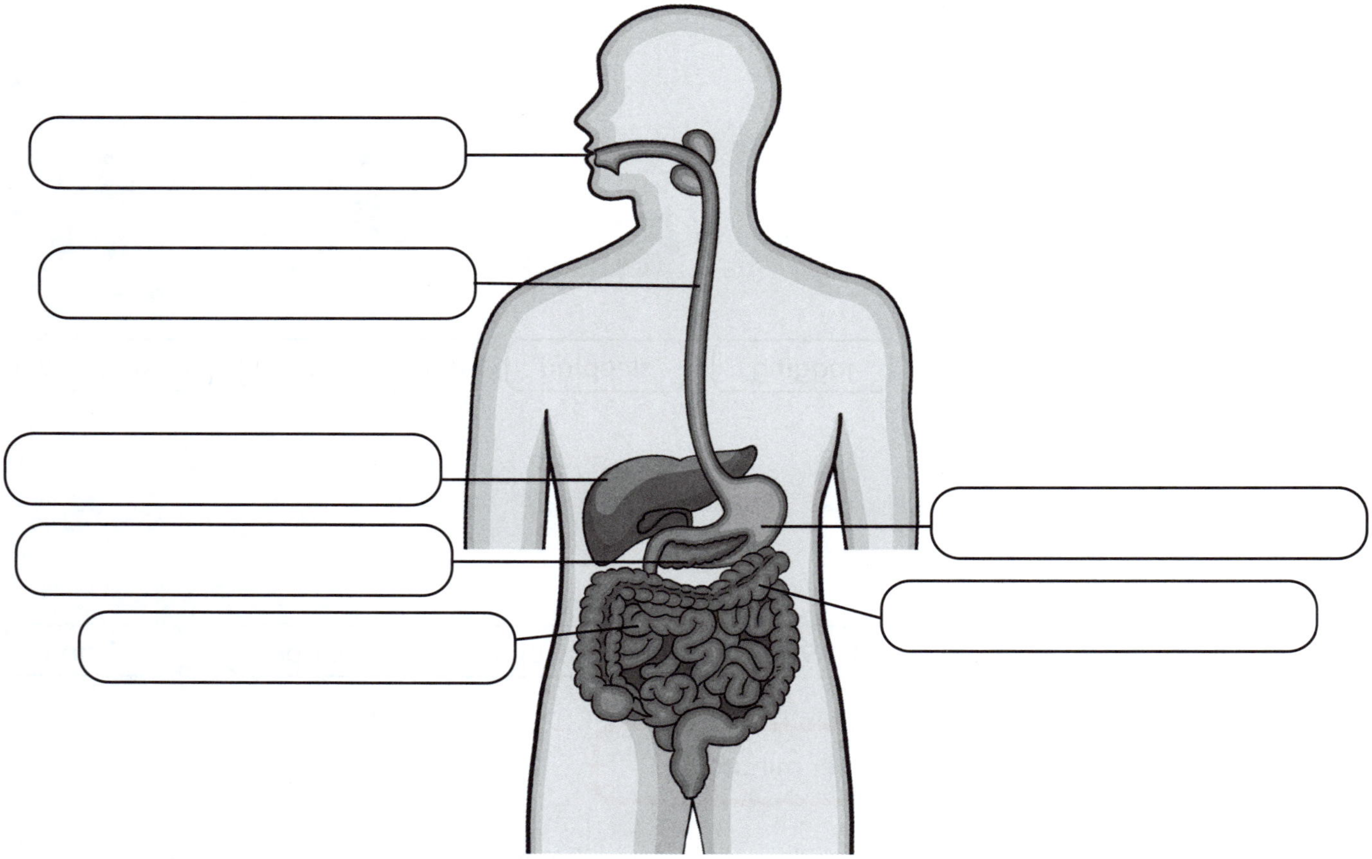

large intestine	liver	mouth	oesophagus
pancreas	small intestine	stomach	

Label the diagram. Use the words in the box.

Stretch zone

Find out the common name for the oesophagus and write it here:

____

Breaking down food

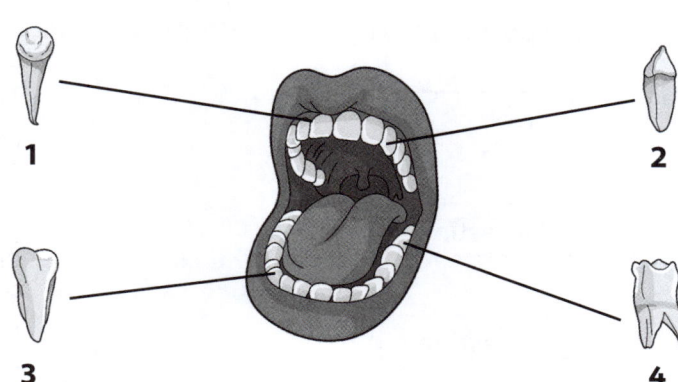

1 Which number shows a tooth that is used for cutting into food?

_____

2 Which number shows a tooth that is used to bite into food?

_____

3 Which numbers show teeth that are used to grind food?

_____

_____

Stretch zone

Find out which types of teeth are called incisors, canines, pre-molars and molars. Find them in your mouth.

Draw a picture of each, labelling each one.

4 Teeth can be damaged and worn away if they are not looked after.

Research and write down two ways that you can look after your teeth.

Absorbing nutrients and water

How nutrients enter the blood

1 Link the part of the digestive system to its function.

liver	This part is where food is chewed and ground up into smaller pieces and an enzyme is added.
small intestine	Food that hasn't been taken into the blood enters here and then out of the body.
large intestine	Enzymes are added and the food passes into the blood here.
stomach	This is where food is mixed and churned and acid and enzymes are added.
mouth	This tube links the mouth with the stomach.
oesophagus	This part makes bile to help break down fats. It also removes harmful substances from the blood.

2 Why is water easily absorbed into the body?

3 Write a short story to describe the journey that food takes after it enters the mouth. Explain how the food is broken down and where this happens. Include the words: nutrients, teeth, enzymes and absorption.

Investigating surface area and absorption

 This activity supports the investigation on page 55 of your Student Book.
You are going to investigate how surface area affects the rate of absorption.

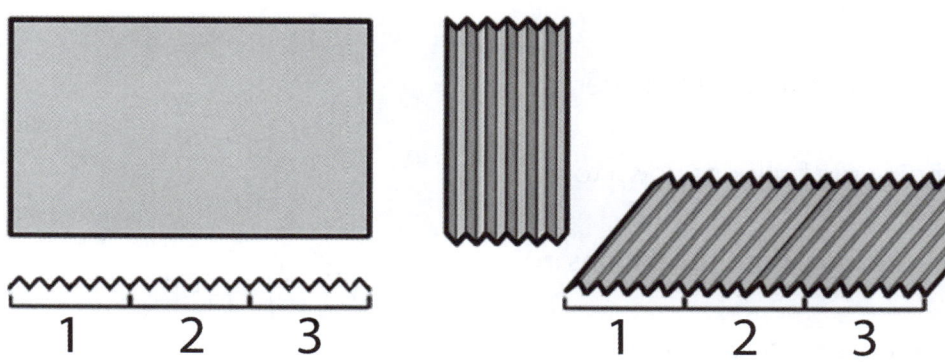

1   Collect four pieces paper. They must be the same size.

2   Find the area of each piece of paper.

> **Remember:** To calculate the area, you multiply length by width.

The surface area of each flat piece of paper is: _____

3   Fold three of the pieces of paper into a concertina. Use the diagram above to help you.

What is the surface area of each folded piece of paper? _____

4   Lay the folded pieces of paper over the flat piece. Make sure they don't overlap.

What is the total area of the three folded pieces of paper? _____

5   How has folding the paper helped you to increase the surface area of the paper? _____

_____

_____

Model the function of the kidney

Some students in your class will model the kidney and some students will model the blood.

Your teacher will set out the room so it looks like the diagram.

Kidney people

- If you are holding the cardboard, you are the filter part of the kidney.
- If you are sitting on a chair, pass balloons down to the end.
- If you are holding the plastic bag, put the balloons in the bag.
- If you are sitting in seat X, pass every alternate water balloon back to the blood.

Blood people

- Pick up a balloon and walk around the blood vessel until you reach the cardboard filter.
- If your balloon fits through the holes, pass it into the kidney.
- If your balloon does not fit through the holes, take it back to the box and pick up another balloon.
- After a few minutes empty the plastic bag. This is what happens when the body gets rid of liquid waste (urine).

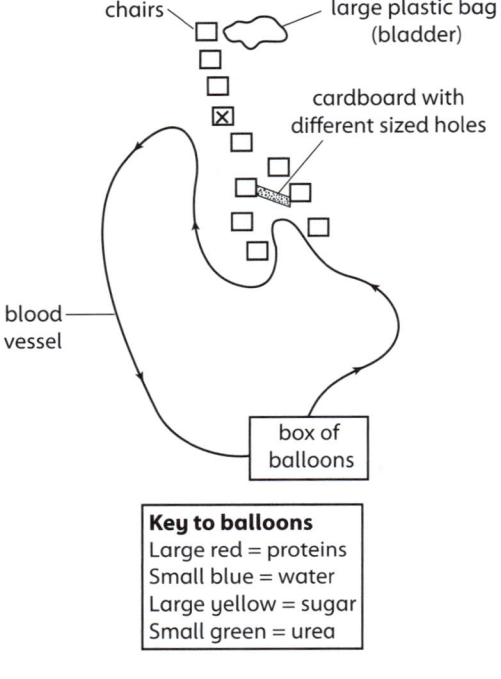

Key to balloons
Large red = proteins
Small blue = water
Large yellow = sugar
Small green = urea

1 What does the model urine contain? _____

2 What is left in the box? _____

Notice that the kidney gets rid of things the body does not want and it keeps vital chemicals.

3 Why is it important that the kidney does not get rid of all of the water in your body?

How the urinary system works

1 Label the diagram. Use words from the box.

> **bladder   kidney   ureter   urethra**

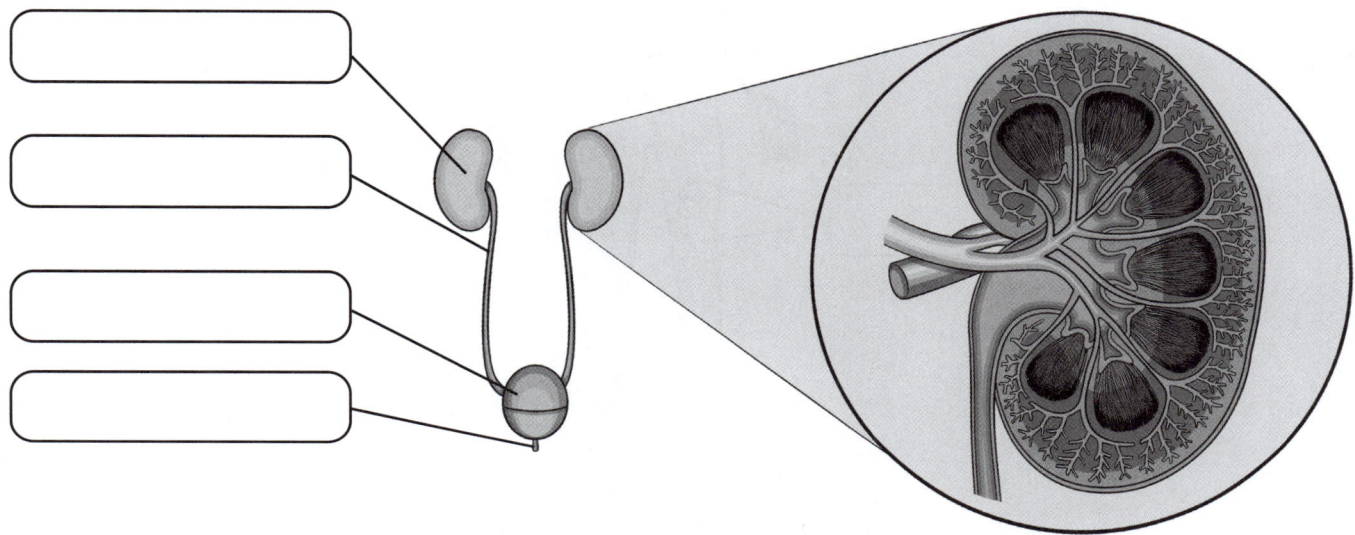

2 Read through the paragraph and use words in the box below to fill in the gaps. You can use each word more than once. Research any gaps you cannot fill. Hint: harmful chemicals or materials are sometimes called poisons.

The _____ help the body to excrete _____. The

_____ have a very good _____ supply. They filter

_____ out of the blood. The _____ are mixed with

water to make _____. This is stored in the _____.

If the _____ are damaged, they cannot remove

_____. Doctors can help by using a machine to filter the

_____. This is called _____.

> **bladder   blood   dialysis   kidneys   poisons   urine**

The brain and nerves

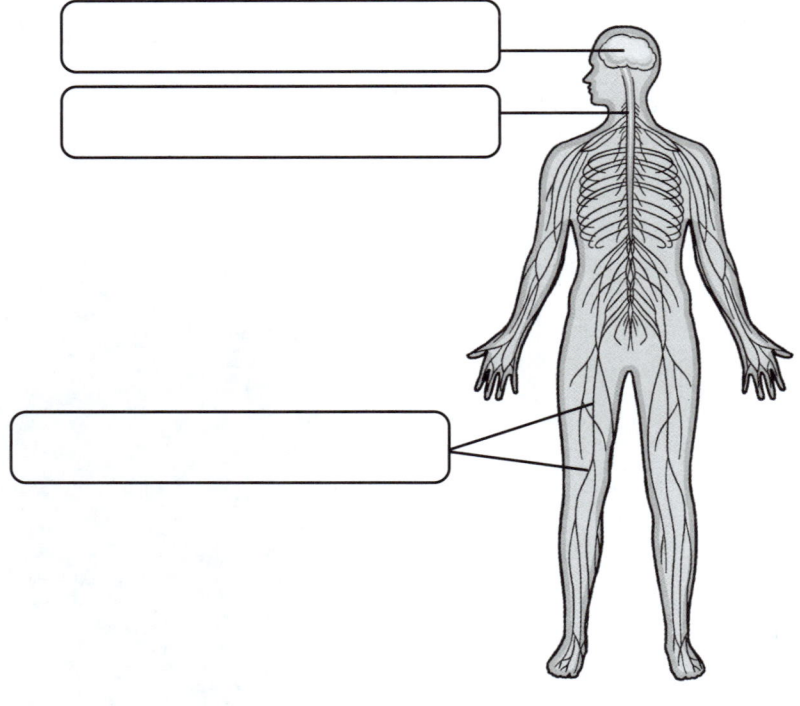

brain   nerves   spinal cord

1   Label the diagram. Use the words in the box.

2   What is the name given to the system that is made up of the brain and spinal cord?

_____

3   Write down three functions of the brain and nerves.

_____

_____

_____

4   Describe two ways in which the brain can be damaged.

_____

_____

How sensitive is your skin?

 This activity supports the investigation on page 59 of your Student Book. You are going to test your nerve endings.

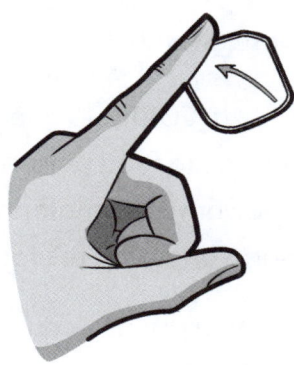

1 Ask a partner to tell you if they feel one or two points.

> **Remember:** If they say one point, open the paperclip so the ends are a bit further apart and test again.
> If they say two points, close the ends slightly and test again.

Warning! You must press very gently. Do not hurt your partner.

2 Record the distance when your partner can feel two points. Use the table below.

Part of the body	Distance where two points were felt (cm)	
	You	**Your partner**
finger		
back of the hand		
forearm		

3 What does your investigation tell you about how far apart nerve endings are in different parts of your body?

4 Why is it important to have very sensitive fingers but not very sensitive forearms?

Infectious diseases and their prevention

Learning about microorganisms

Read the text below. Follow the instructions and answer the questions.

Some microorganisms can cause diseases. Disease-causing microorganisms are called pathogens. Some examples are given below.

- Viruses – such as influenza, COVID-19, measles and smallpox
- Bacteria – such as salmonella food poisoning, anthrax and cholera
- Parasites – such as tapeworm and malaria parasite. These live on or inside the body
- Fungi – such as ringworm and athlete's foot

A person or animal infected with a disease-causing microorganism is called the host. Microorganisms and the diseases they cause can pass from host to host. This is called transmission of a disease. If a disease is passed on like this, it is called an infectious disease.

Microorganisms enter your body from the air, water you drink, food, through cuts in your skin and from contact with infected people. Diseases can also be transmitted from animal hosts to humans and by bites from insects. Animals that spread diseases are called vectors.

1 Circle the word in the text that is the name given to disease-causing microorganisms.

2 Underline the word in the text that is used to describe the person or animal infected with a microorganism.

3 Write down two examples of diseases caused by viruses.

_____ and _____

4 Write down a disease caused by bacteria.

_____

5 Which type of living thing causes athlete's foot?

_____

6 If someone asked you what a parasite is, what would you tell them? Write your answer in the box.

Researching diseases and pathogens

 This activity supports the investigation on page 61 of your Student Book.

You are going to use secondary sources to research diseases.

1 What is a secondary source?

2 Use the table below to record your research findings.

	Type of pathogen			
	Virus	**Bacterium**	**Parasite**	**Fungi**
Name				
Description				
How dangerous is it?				
How is it transmitted?				
How can it be treated?				
How can it be prevented?				
Where in the world does it occur the most?				

3 Use this information to make a poster. Display your poster to make a disease exhibition.

Food labels survey

This activity supports the food labels survey investigation on page 63 of your Student Book.

Labels can be slightly different. Don't let this worry you. Just check to see how much of each food type is in the food.

Check the units – it might be grams per 100 grams or even milligrams. These are one thousand times less than a gram.

1 Study the labels of the food cans, bottles and packets in front of you.

2 Classify the foods into four types: protein rich, carbohydrate rich, fat rich and mineral and vitamin rich.

3 Complete the table below to record your results. Add the units each time.

| Food | Amount of food type | | | | | |
	protein	fat	carbohydrate	sugar	sodium	Which food type is the food rich in?

4 Now plan your healthy meal. Write your ideas below before producing your menu card.

Make your own healthy eating plate

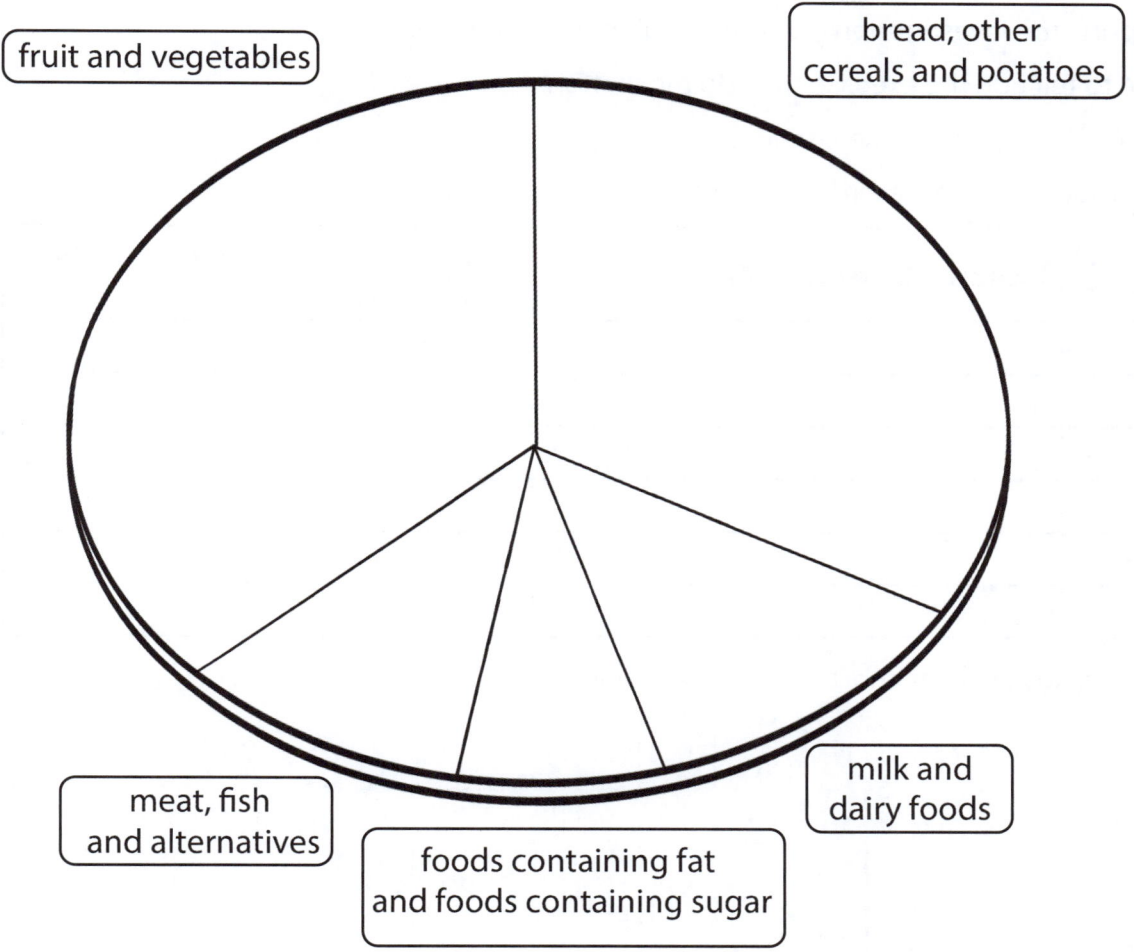

fruit and vegetables

bread, other
cereals and potatoes

meat, fish
and alternatives

foods containing fat
and foods containing sugar

milk and
dairy foods

Think back to what you have eaten in the last 24 hours.

1   Add the foods to the correct part of the blank healthy eating plate.

You can write the names of the foods or draw them.

2   Study your plate.

Decide if it is a healthy balanced diet. This is called evaluation.

3   Write down anything you should consider adding to your diet.

4   Write down anything you should consider eating less of in your diet.

Exercise survey

 This activity supports the investigation on page 64 of your Student Book.

1 Ask six people to tell you the exercise they do most often.

Find out how long they do the exercise for.

2 Complete the table below to record your findings.

Person	Exercise done most often	Time spent doing the exercise per week (minutes)

3 Present your findings as a bar chart. Use the axes below to help you.

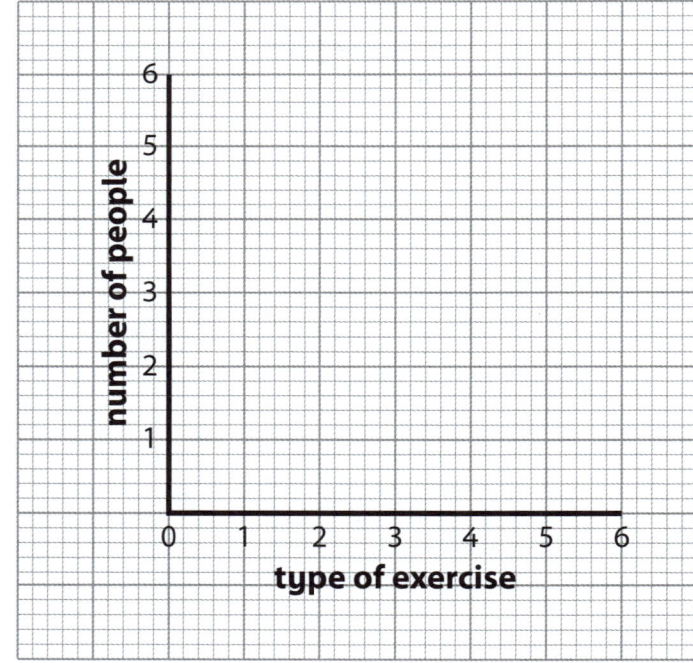

4 Which was the most popular type of exercise? _____

5 What is the average time spent on exercise per week? _____

6 Now design a poster or presentation to share your findings.

Remember to include some pictures to show examples of the types of exercise.

Personal hygiene

1 Study the pictures below.

2 For each picture, name the object. Explain why it is important for personal hygiene.

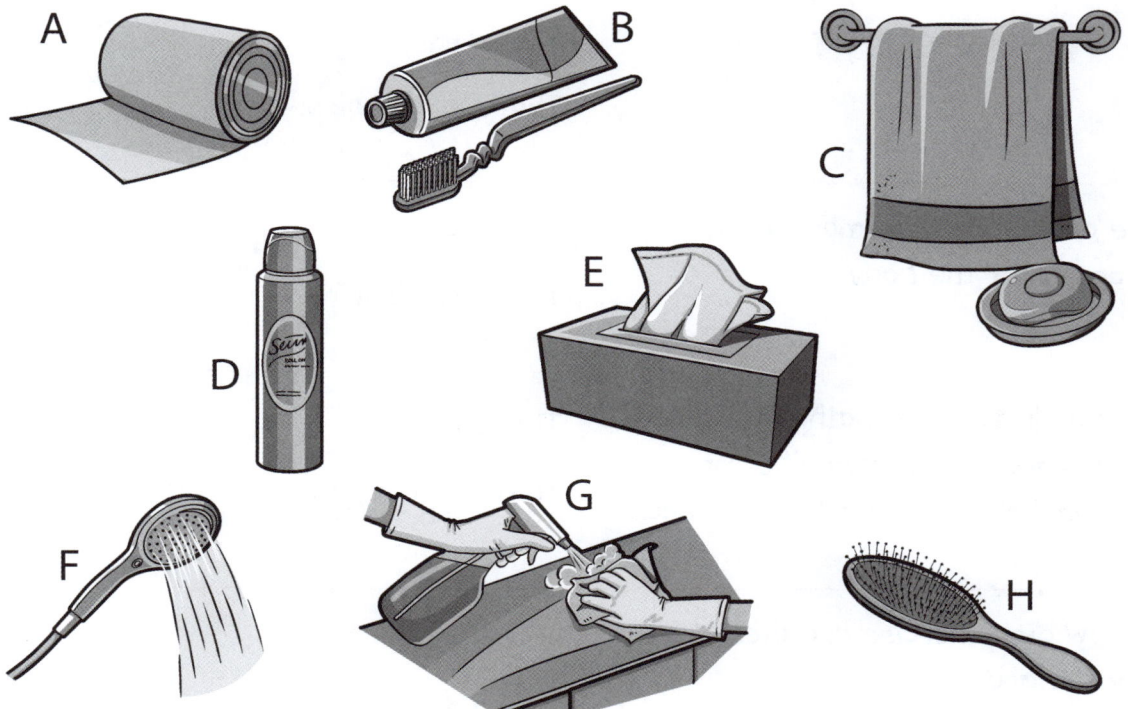

Letter	Name of object	Why is this important for personal hygiene?

What went well

1 Think about what you have learned.

2 Talk to a friend about something that went well in this unit.

3 Tick ✓ the boxes to rate yourself.

I can identify the position of major organs in the body.	That's easy. ☐ That's challenging. ☐	Pages 44–45
I can describe and explain the main functions of the major organs of the body.	That's easy. ☐ That's challenging. ☐	Pages 46–59
I can name the main types of pathogens that cause infectious diseases and describe some of the ways of preventing the spread of infectious diseases.	That's easy. ☐ That's challenging. ☐	Pages 60–61
I can explain how diet, exercise and lifestyle affect the way the body functions.	That's easy. ☐ That's challenging. ☐	Pages 62–65

If you want to know more or need to check, go back to the pages in your Student Book.

 **Investigate like a scientist**

Making a model lung

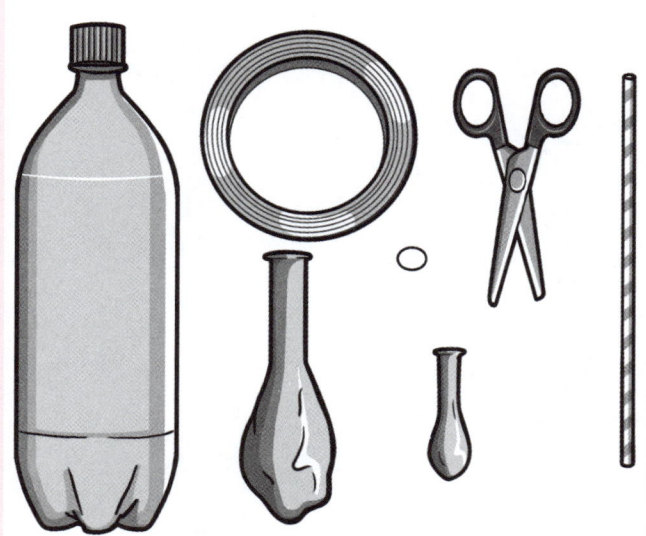
step 1

step 2

You are going to design and construct a model lung.

Use the equipment shown in the left-hand diagram.

Use the right-hand diagram to help you construct your lung.

Once you have made your model lung try to get the lung to inflate (fill with air).

 1 Explain what you did to make your model lung inflate (fill up) and deflate (empty).

    a To inflate the lung I _____

    _____ .

    b To deflate the lung I _____

    _____ .

2 Hold your hand just beneath your ribs at the front. Breathe in and out deeply.

    What do you feel? _____

    _____

 **Stretch zone** ➤

Find out where the diaphragm is and what it does.

Key words

Complete the crossword puzzle.

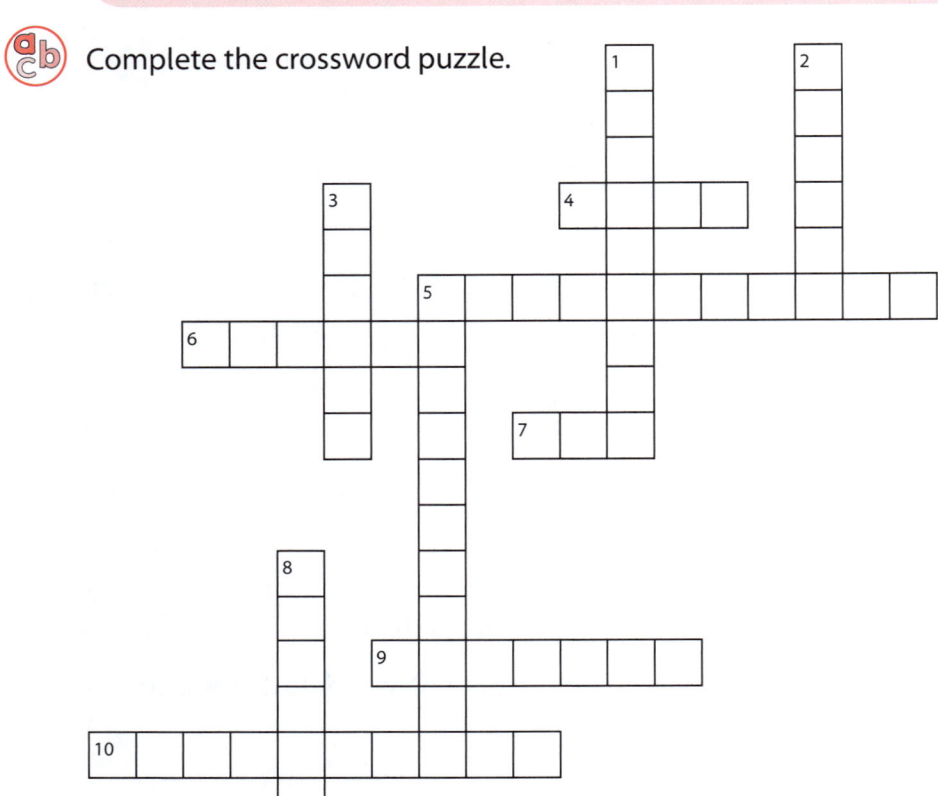

Across

4 This can come from a torch and is a collection of rays.

5 A material that lets most of the light through.

6 A shiny object that lets us see ourselves.

7 A line that shows how light travels.

9 This means to bounce back.

10 The outline of a person that you can draw round.

Down

1 This describes how much light there is.

2 A material that lets no light through.

3 This word describes where something starts from.

5 A material that lets some light through.

8 A shape cast by blocking light.

Rainbows

1 The light from the Sun contains all the colours of a rainbow.

Colour in the rainbow and label each colour.

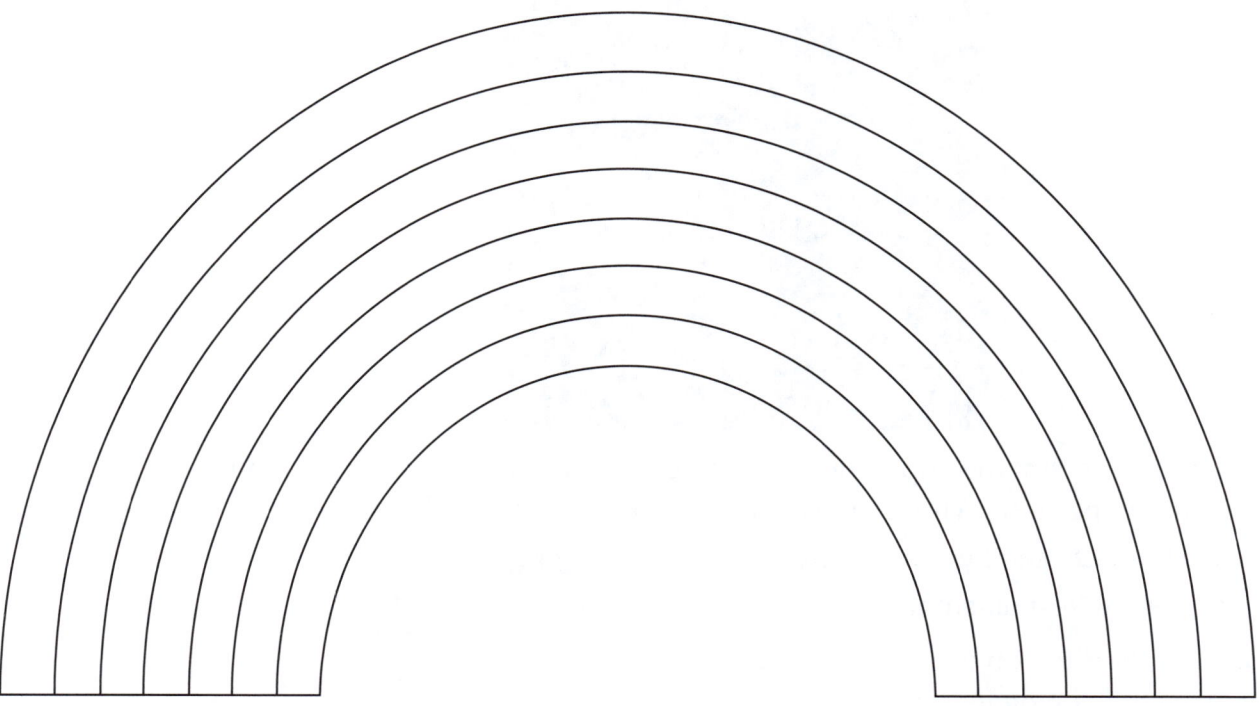

2 Label the following on the diagram below. Use the words in the box. One has been done for you.

Sun   raindrops   ~~white light~~

white light

Is there a link between sight and taste?

Look at the photograph. It shows food presented on plates. The food is made to look attractive.

Scientists believe that the appearance of food can influence how we taste it. You can test this hypothesis. A hypothesis is an idea that hasn't been fully proven.

 Is there a link between sight and taste?

You are going to test different foods.

 **Warning!** Tell your teacher if you have any food allergies. Why is this important?

1 Sit on a chair. Put on a blindfold or close your eyes if you prefer.

2 You will be handed four different foods. Eat them without being able to see them.

3 Try to identify the flavour of each food.

4 Now eat the foods as you look at them. Record any differences in taste you noticed.

5 Take it in turns until everyone has tried different foods with and without being able to see them.

6 Write a short summary to give your ideas about any possible links between sight and taste.

How important is sight?

You can work with a partner or in a small group for this activity.

Take it in turns to wear a blindfold. You can choose to close your eyes if you prefer.

Move around the room. Your partner or another member of your group will help you and make sure you are safe.

1 Record what it feels like to move around this way. What sounds can you hear?

_____

_____

2 Now carry a walking stick and tap it on the floor and in front of you.

Did your hearing help you to find your way around?   **yes**   **no**

3 Try the same activity in a much larger space – such as a hall.

Record what it feels like. What sounds can you hear?

_____

_____

Tricking your eyes

Work with a partner.

1 Look at the picture.

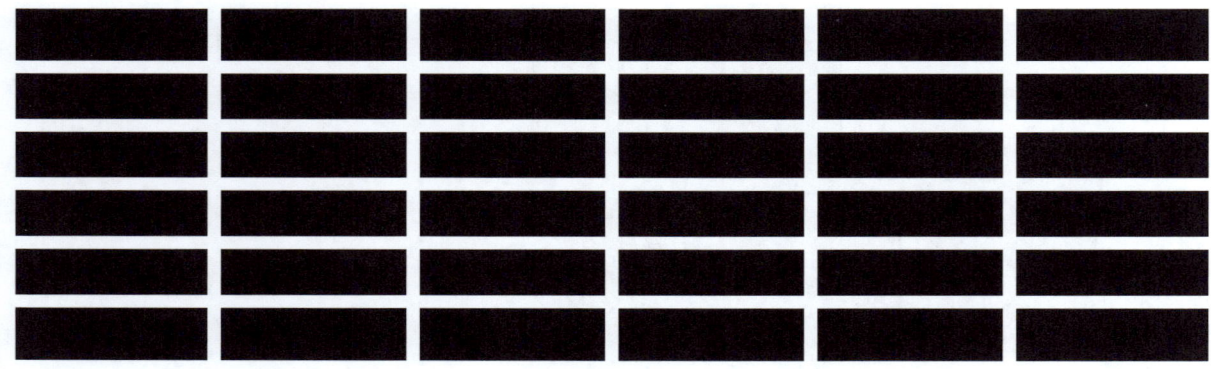

   a Can you see any circles?   **yes**   **no**

   b What colour are they?   _____

   c Discuss with your partner what you can see.

2 Look at the two sets of lines. Which horizontal line is longer, line A or line B? _____

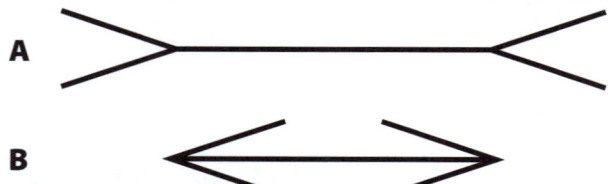

A

B

3 Use a ruler to measure the length of the horizontal lines.

Line A: _____ centimetres

Line B: _____ centimetres

Did your eyes trick you?

Visual tricks like these are called optical illusions.

If your brain does not get a full picture, it tries to fill in any gaps. Normally this is very useful – but sometimes it tricks us and makes up things that are not really there.

Stretch zone

Research three more examples of optical illusions. Print them out and challenge other people to see if they trick their eyes.

Making a science animated film

You are going to make an animated film using post-it notes or a small notepad.

1 Draw two circles in the bottom right-hand corner of the top post-it note.

2 Draw two more identical circles in the bottom left-hand corner of the second post-it note.

3 Repeat this process until you have drawn on 10 post-it notes.

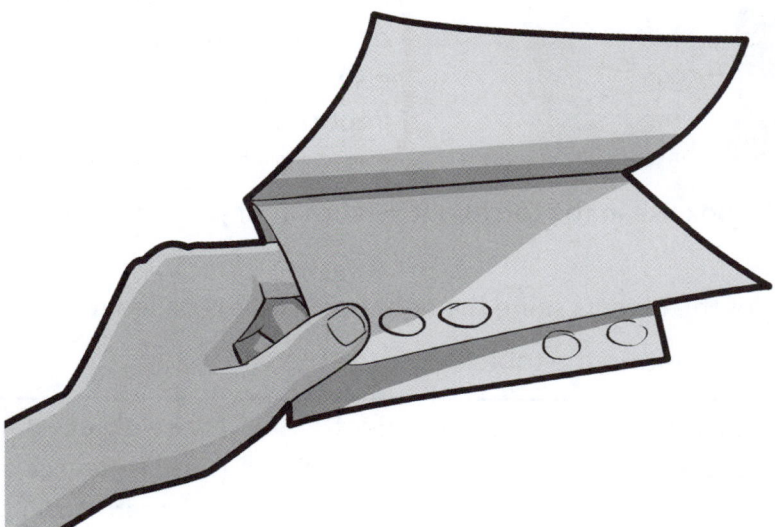

4 Hold the edge where the notes are stuck together. Flick the notes from the loose end.

What do the circles do?

You should see that they appear to move.

What is your hypothesis (idea) about why this happens?

You can make an animation using this technique. Choose an idea in science that involves changes – for example, water and water vapour moving in the water cycle or a butterfly life cycle.

5 Draw the changes on a number of post-it notes and flick them to make your animation.

6 Film the animation with a smartphone or digital camera. Perhaps you can have an animated film festival to share your creative ideas.

Shining back

 This activity supports the investigation on page 74 of your Student Book.

Which materials are good and poor reflectors?

An adult will make the room darker. You are going to shine a torch onto six different objects.

Warning! Do not shine a torch directly at someone else. Discuss why this is important.

1 Predict what you think the objects will look like in the torchlight. Record your predictions for each of the objects in the table below.

Are the objects dull or shiny? Will any of the objects shine the light back? This is called reflection.

2 Observe what happens and record your results in the table.

Name of object	What material is the object made from?	Predict if the object will reflect light.	Is the object shiny or dull in torchlight?	Is the object a good reflector or poor reflector?

3 How accurate were your predictions?

Artificial light

Sources of light can be natural. Other sources of light can be artificial.

1 Write down one example of a natural light source. _____

2 Write down some sources of artificial light. You can use ones you can see and ones that you know about.

_____

_____

3 Look at the artificial sources of light that you have listed.

Explain why a natural source of light cannot be used.

_____

_____

Stretch zone

Research how lamps and torches have been developed over the past 200 years.

The mirrored image

 This activity supports Part 2 of the investigation on page 77 of your Student Book.

How can you prove that a mirrored image is back to front?

1 Place an object in front of a mirror. Point to the left side of the object and look in the mirror. What do you see?

2 Point to the right side of the object and look in the mirror. What do you see?

3 Follow the path of Star A with a pencil. Draw between the two outer lines and do not touch the sides. Now collect a small mirror. Look at Star B in the mirror and try to draw around it between the two lines. Do not look at Star B, only look at its mirrored image.

Was it easier to draw around Star A or Star B? Why?

Star A

Star B

Mirror writing

1 **a** Try to read this sentence.

> ‎.Mirrors reflect light.

The famous scientist, Leonardo da Vinci, wrote his notes using a mirror

b Write what the sentence says. _____

c Now hold the sentence up to a mirror.
Were you correct?   **yes**   **no**

2 Use a mirror to create your own secret writing. Write a sentence to describe some science you have done at school. Look in the mirror as you write so that your writing is mirror writing.

My mirror writing

3 Ask your classmates whether they can read your mirror writing.

Then give them a mirror so they can find out what you have learned.

4 **a** Draw an object in the classroom while looking at it in a mirror.

My mirror drawing

b How is the real object different from its image in the mirror? _____

_____

Uses of reflection

Making a periscope

 This activity supports the investigation on page 79 of your Student Book.

You will need: two small mirrors, a shoe box or other narrow box made of thin card, scissors, sticky tape.

Use the diagrams to help you make your periscope.

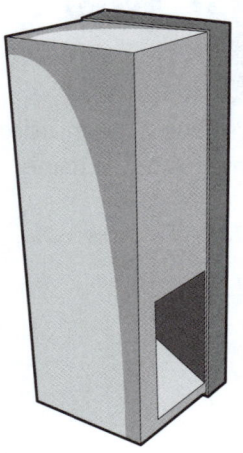 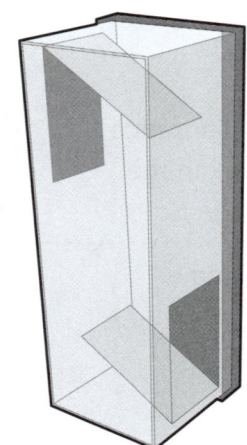

Warning! You can use pieces from an old CD if you do not have any small mirrors.

Ask an adult to cut the CDs. Be careful – mirrors and cut CDs have sharp edges.

1 Cut flaps so that two small mirrors can be placed inside the box.

2 Stick the mirrors inside the box, fixing them at a 45° angle.

3 Now test your periscope.

   a Can you see around corners?   **yes**   **no**

   b Can you see over objects?   **yes**   **no**

4 Why do the mirrors have to be at a 45° angle?

Guiding light

You are going to make an obstacle course to test how light travels.

You will need: a torch, a shoe box or other narrow box made of thin card, scissors, small mirrors, some pieces of card.

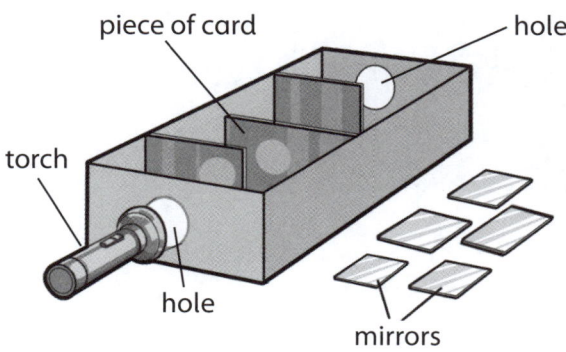

1 Cut a hole in one end of the shoe box, so that it is just big enough to fit the end of a torch into.

2 Cut another hole in the other end of the shoe box for the light to travel out of.

3 Stick pieces of card to the sides of the shoe box to make a pathway or maze structure.

4 Now replace the lid of the shoe box and put the torch into the opening.

Switch on the torch.

5 Do you predict that any of the light will come out of the other end of the shoe box?

Explain your answer.

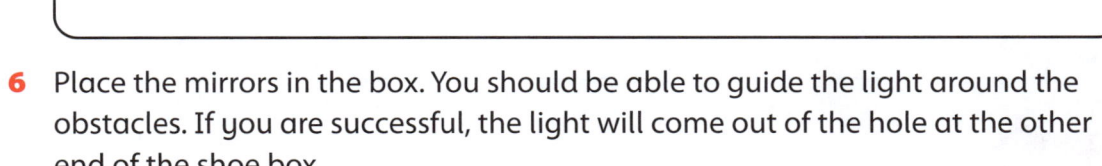

6 Place the mirrors in the box. You should be able to guide the light around the obstacles. If you are successful, the light will come out of the hole at the other end of the shoe box.

Ray diagrams

Mirrors and design

Mirrors are used for making the insides and outsides of houses and buildings look bigger and brighter. Inside buildings this is a part of the interior design.

 Find examples of mirrors used in interior design.

1   Use magazines or the internet to find examples of mirrors being used in interior design.

2   Do any of the mirrors help to make the room bigger or brighter?

   Draw or cut out and stick an example in the box.

3   Find the main source of light in your picture above.

   Draw a ray diagram onto the picture to show how the light travels from the light source and where it travels.

4   Explain how the mirror makes the room bigger or brighter.

   _____

   _____

 Stretch zone

Research how mirrors can be used to make life safer.

Make a pinhole camera

The pinhole camera is one of the earliest types of camera. You are going to make your own camera.

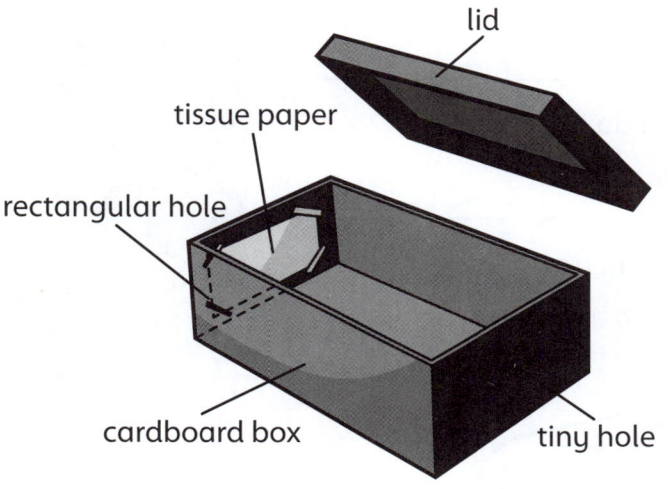

lid

tissue paper

rectangular hole

cardboard box

tiny hole

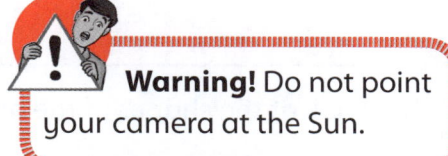

Warning! Do not point your camera at the Sun.

1. Find a cardboard box such as a shoe box.

2. Cut out a rectangle from one of the smaller sides.

3. Glue or tape a strip of thin tissue paper over the hole to make a screen.

4. Make a tiny 'pinhole' in the middle of the side opposite your screen.

    Make this hole as small as possible. You can make it a bit bigger later if you need to.

5. Place the lid of the box back on to keep the light out of your camera.

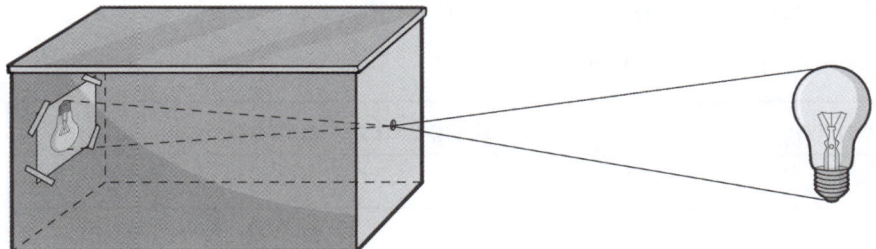

6. Point the pinhole at a light source such as a light bulb or a candle.

    If you cannot see anything on the outside of the screen, make your pinhole slightly bigger.

7. Take your camera outside and point it at bright objects.

    What do you notice about the images of the objects?

Light changing direction

Having fun with mirrors

1 Look at the photograph.

   a What has happened to the mirror image?

   _____

   b Look at the shapes of the mirror. What do you notice?

   _____

2 How can you change the reflection from a mirror?

You are going to use some flexible mirrors or mirrors on a roll.

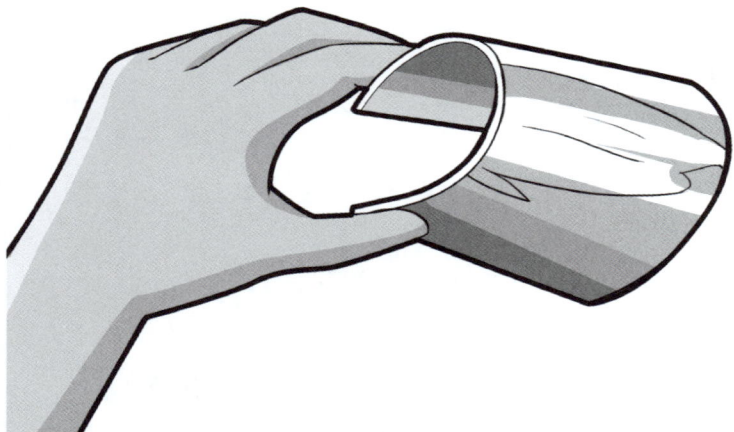

   a Bend the mirror in different ways. Observe the reflections.

   b Record your findings in the table below.

Shape of mirror	Shape of reflection

Stretch zone

Look for some examples of shaped mirrors. Research why some are called concave and some are called convex.

Does light travel in straight lines?

You are going to use three pieces of card and a torch or light bulb to investigate how light travels.

You will need: three pieces of thick card, a hole punch or pencil, modelling clay or reusable adhesive, a torch or lit bulb, a small area of blank wall or a large piece of card covered with paper.

1   Make a small hole in the centre of each piece of card.

Use a hole punch or carefully push a pencil through.

Make sure the hole is in the same position on all the cards.

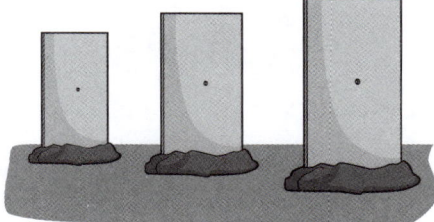

2   Stand the cards up using modelling clay or reusable adhesive.

3   Shine a torch or a lit bulb onto the cards.

4   Investigate how to arrange the cards so that the light passes through all the holes and shines onto the wall or a paper screen behind.

5   How did you have to line up the holes? _____

_____

6   Does this show that light travels in a straight line? Explain your answer.

_____

_____

7   Draw your apparatus. Show the light as a beam leaving the light source and hitting the wall or paper screen.

Investigating refraction

 You are going to use refraction to see a hidden object.

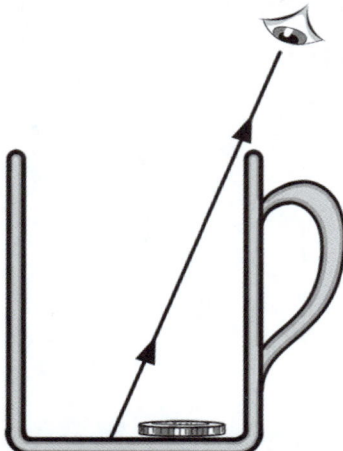

Coin is invisible

1 Place a coin inside a cup near to one side. Stand back slightly, so you cannot see the coin.

2 Ask your partner to stand in the same place. Check if they can see the coin.

3 Now slowly add water to the cup. Observe what happens.

4 Use your knowledge of refraction to explain why adding water makes a difference.

5 Draw ray lines on the diagram below to show your ideas.

Stretch zone

Research how refraction can make objects underwater appear much closer than they are. Draw some examples and display your drawings.

Colour investigation

You may have read a book using a torch. Think about the colours you could see in the book.

You are going to investigate colours that are reflected from objects.

1 Shine the white light from a torch onto coloured objects.

2 Record the colours reflected. Use the table below

Colour of object	Colour you see

3 Find a black object. What colour do you see when you shine white light on it?

_____

4 Now cover the torch with a coloured acetate or filter.

5 Choose some coloured objects, such as a piece of lego or a small model.

Shine the torch at the objects. What colour do they appear?

6 Record your results.

Colour of object	Colour of light	Colour you see

 7 Does the colour of the object you see look different in different coloured light?

Can we see through it?

Does it let light through or block light?

1 Complete the sentences using the words in the box below. You will need to use each word more than once.

An object that does not let light through is _____. We cannot see through

_____ materials.

An object that lets a lot of light through is _____. We can see clearly through

_____ materials. The glass in windows is a _____ material.

Some objects let a little light through. These are made from _____ materials.

We can see shapes on the other side of _____ materials but not very clearly.

Coloured and frosted glass are examples of _____ materials.

> **opaque   translucent   transparent**

2 Look at the pictures. The student is looking through a different material in each one.
Label each picture with the correct word from the box to describe the material.

a [ ]

b [ ]

c [ ]

Translucent, transparent and opaque objects

1 a Talk to your partner about the different types of material shown in the picture. Use the words 'translucent', 'transparent' and 'opaque' to describe whether or not they let light through.

  b Talk about materials that you can see in the room where you are.

2 Survey some different materials.

  a Find two opaque objects.

- Explain to the person you are working with why you know this object is made from opaque material.
- How can you prove that a material is opaque?

  b Find two translucent objects.

- How can you prove that each object is made from a translucent material?

  c Find two transparent objects.

- Draw the two transparent objects you have found.
- Label your drawings to explain what the objects are used for.

Making shadows

Does it make a good shadow?

1 Talk to your partner about how shadows are made.

- What kind of material makes the best shadow?
- Why does a transparent material not make a good shadow? What happens to the light?

2 Which materials make a good shadow?

a Find five objects that you can test.

b Predict whether each object will make a good shadow or a bad shadow.

c Fill in the table with your predictions.

Object	Prediction: good shadow or bad shadow?	Result: good shadow or bad shadow?

3 Now test your prediction.

- Use a torch or lamp as a source of light.
- Use a white piece of paper or a white wall as a screen.
- Shine the light on the object with the wall or screen behind it.

4 Did the objects cast shadows? Fill in the table with the results.

5 Did any of the objects make good shadows? _____

6 Did any objects surprise you? _____

Stretch zone

Think about where you see shadows around the school. How does this link to your investigation?

Investigating translucent and opaque materials

This activity supports the investigation on page 88 of your Student Book.

1. Choose three translucent materials and three opaque materials.

2. Plan how to test how much light passes through the material.

   You can use shadows to help you.

   If the shadow is darker, then more light has been blocked.

3. Write your plan in the space below.

   Draw a diagram of the equipment.

4. Are the shadows made by the opaque and translucent materials the same?

   _____

5. Draw pictures to show the shadow a translucent object would make and the shadow an opaque object would make. Use the boxes below.

Translucent	Opaque

Stretch zone

Suggest one situation where a translucent material would be better than an opaque one.

_____

_____

Shadow games

Making shadows

This activity supports the shadow puppets investigation on page 90 of your Student Book. There are different ways to make a shadow puppet.

You will need: your hands, a source of light (for example a torch).

1 Hold your hand in front of the torch.

2 Look at the shadow it casts on a surface. A clear white wall makes a good surface.

3 Try to make the following animals and shapes to help you.

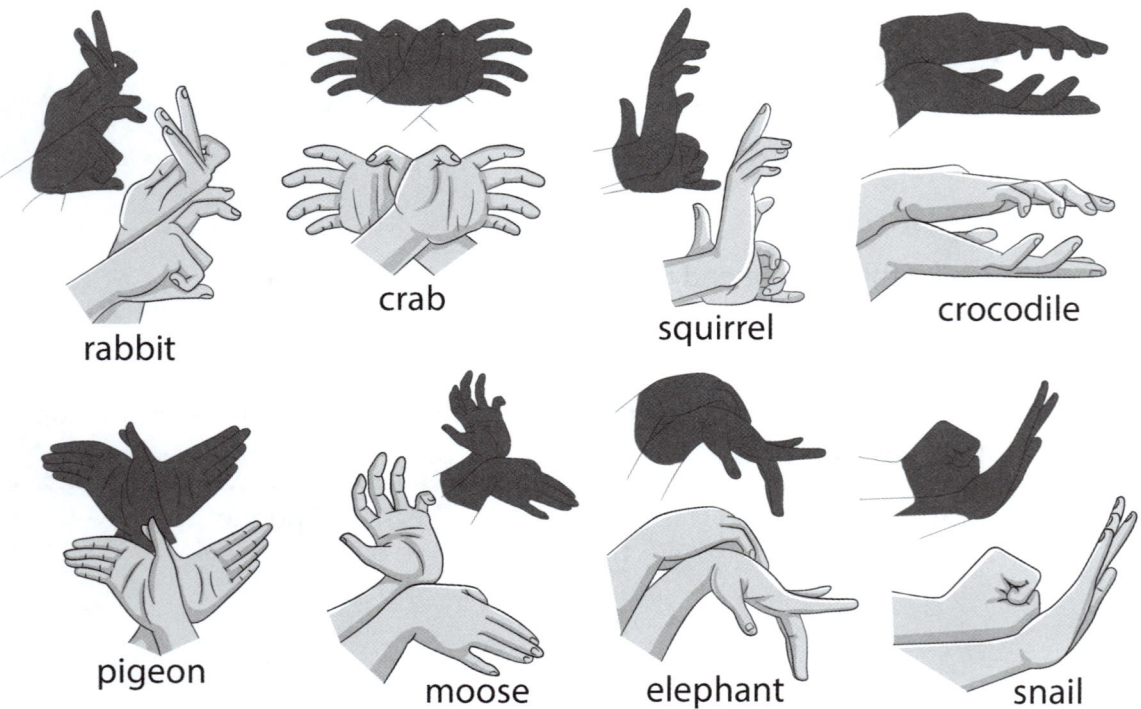

rabbit

crab

squirrel

crocodile

pigeon

moose

elephant

snail

You might be able to create some of your own.

4 Work with a partner to write a story using your hand puppets.

5 Act out the story for the rest of your class.

Making silhouettes

This activity supports the student silhouettes investigation on page 91 of your Student Book.

This picture shows the silhouette of the profile of a girl

1 Talk to your partner about silhouettes.

2 Make a silhouette.

Ask someone to take part in this activity. You will make a silhouette of their profile from the side.

You will need: a sharp pencil, a large piece of paper, a light source (a torch or lamp), a piece of black card, scissors.

3 Ask the person to sit about one metre from a wall or screen. They must sit sideways so you can make a shadow of their profile.

Ask the person to sit very still.

4 Tape a piece of paper to the wall or screen. Make sure it is in the right position so you can see the person's shadow on the paper.

Ask permission before you tape the paper to the wall or screen.

5 Turn off the light in the room. Close the curtains or blinds. The room needs to be dark.

6 Shine a light onto the side of the person's face.

7 Draw around the shadow that is cast onto the paper.

8 Stick the piece of paper onto black card. Carefully cut out the silhouette.

Tell the person you have drawn that this is how Étienne de Silhouette made pictures of people in the 1700s.

Growing and shrinking shadows

Investigate the size of shadows

Look at the diagrams. They show two objects with a source of light shining on them.
The shadow of each object is cast onto the screen.

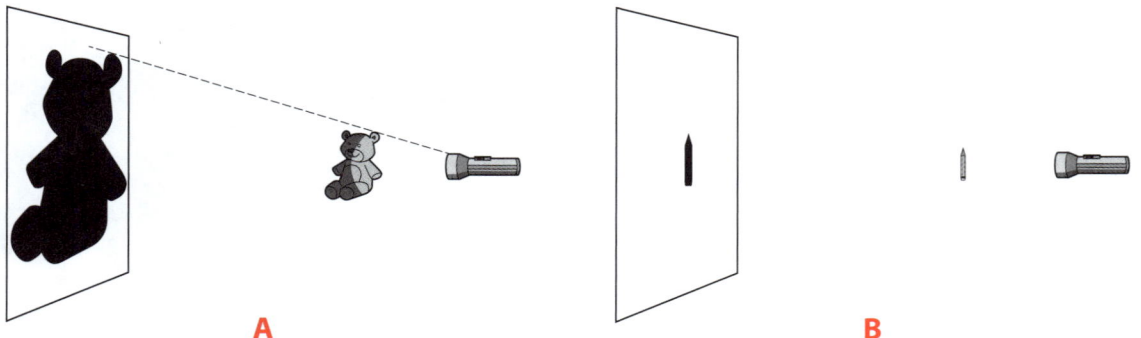

A   B

1 Draw a straight line from the top of the light source, across the top of the object, to the screen.
One has been done for you.

2 Draw another straight line from the bottom of the light source to the screen.

3 Measure the length of the shadow cast onto the screen by each object. Record your measurements.

Object A: _____ mm

Object B: _____ mm

4 Which object casts a bigger shadow? _____

5 Do bigger objects cast bigger shadows?

   a Find two objects that are similar but different sizes.

   b Measure and record the length of each object.

   c Use a light source to cast each object's shadow onto a piece of paper.

   d Measure from the top to the bottom of each shadow. Record your measurements.

Object	Length of object (cm)	Length of shadow (cm)

   e Does the bigger object cast a bigger shadow?   **yes**   **no**

Moving shadow puppets

This activity supports the investigation on page 93 of your Student Book. Use the shadow puppets you have made. You are going to explore how to make these shadow puppets appear to move.

1 One person should hold the puppet in front of the source of light.

   They should try to hold the puppet as still as they can.

2 Observe what happens to the shadow puppet.

3 Move the torch to make the shadow puppet move.

4 Repeat the investigation, but this time move the light source 5, 10 and 20 centimetres to the right. Measure how much the shadows move. Do the same again, this time moving the light source to the left. Record your results below.

Direction the light source moves	How much the light source was moved (centimetres)	How much the shadow moves (centimetres)
To the right	5	
	10	
	20	
To the left	5	
	10	
	20	

Tracking moving shadows

Shadow hide and seek

You are going to use shadows to play a game of 'Shadow hide and seek'.

Play the game in a small group or with the whole class.

1   One student in your group is the seeker.

2   The seeker must close their eyes and count to 20.

3   While the seeker is counting, the other students must hide. They must stand so they cannot be seen but their shadow can be.

4   When the seeker has finished counting they can turn around.

5   The seeker must look for people's shadows. When they see a shadow, they must guess who the person is by the shape of the shadow.

6   The seeker says the name of the person they think it is. If the seeker is correct, that person is out.

7   How many people can the seeker guess correctly?

Take turns to be the seeker and the hiders.

Does the darkness of shadows change during the day?

You are going to investigate whether the darkness of shadows changes during the day.

You will need to take measurements in the morning, midday and afternoon.

1 One person should stand outside in the Sun.

   • The rest of the team make observations about the shadow cast.
   • They take photographs to show how dark the shadow is.

2 Record the observations in a table like the one below.

Time of day	Observations	Photograph
morning		
midday		
afternoon		

3 Write a conclusion about your observations. Answer the questions to help you.

   a Did the darkness of the shadow change throughout the day?

   _____

   b When was the shadow the darkest?

   _____

   c When was the shadow the lightest?

   _____

4 Would this be a fair test if the person making the shadow was different each time?

   _____

Stretch zone

Are your results reliable? What could you do to make them as reliable as possible? Explain your answer.

Make a sundial

 You are going to make and test a sundial.

You will need: a paper plate, a pencil.

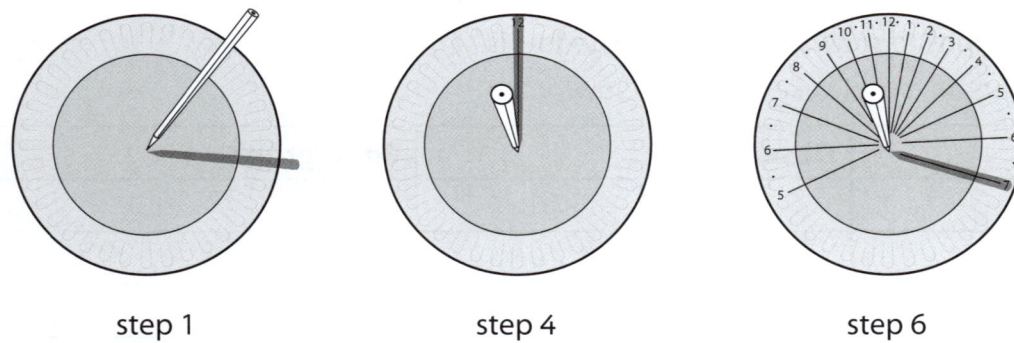

step 1   step 4   step 6

1   Carefully push the pencil through the centre of the plate. An adult may help with this.

2   Write the time on the edge of the plate. For example, if it is midday write 12. Draw a straight line from the centre of the plate to the number.

3   Take the plate outside. Place it in the sunshine, on the ground or a flat surface. The pencil will cast its shadow onto your plate.

4   Turn the plate so that the shadow falls on the line you have drawn.

5   One hour later, go outside again. Draw a line where the shadow is and write the time.

6   Every hour, predict where you think the next line will be. Then go outside to check. Draw the line and write the time.

7   At the end of the day, predict where you think the line will be early the next morning.

8   Test your finished sundial throughout the next day.

Is your sundial accurate in telling the time?   **yes**   **no**

Stretch zone

Evaluate your sundial. Discuss some ways to improve it with other students in your class.

In the next activity, you are going to make an improved model and test it for a few days.

Telling the time with shadows

1 Describe how you made a sundial to your partner.

- Explain how you used shadows to tell the time.
- Tell them how you turned the sundial at the beginning of the investigation so the shadow pointed to the right time.
- Talk about the improvements you would like to make to the sundial.

2 Now you will make and test an improved sundial.

a Plan how to make an improved model for a sundial.

- What equipment will you need?
- Will you use the same method?

b Write details or draw your improved design in the box.

3 Test your improved sundial for a few days. Find out if it tells the time accurately.

You can record your results in tables like the ones below.

| Day _____ | Time of day | | | | | | | |
| | Time on sundial | | | | | | | |

| Day _____ | Time of day | | | | | | | |
| | Time on sundial | | | | | | | |

4 Compare the time of day to the time shown on the sundial.

a Is the sundial more accurate at some times of day than others?

_____

b Did your improvements work?

_____

Light intensity

Measuring light intensity

 This activity supports the investigation on page 99 of your Student Book.

Recall how you can use a solar-powered calculator as a light meter.

1 Plan an investigation to compare a torch, a candle, the Sun and a table lamp. Find two other sources of your own to compare.

Use a solar-powered calculator and tissue paper in your plan

2 In the space below, use instructions and diagrams to help others carry out your investigation.

Which light source will be brightest?

You are going to predict which light source will be the brightest. The brightest light source will need the most sheets of tissue paper to stop the calculator display working.

Some examples you could try are:

- torchlight
- a table lamp
- a room light
- sunlight
- moonlight.

1 Which light source do you think will be brightest?

I think _____ will need the most sheets of tissue paper to stop the calculator display working.

2 Use the solar-powered calculator to find out which light source is the brightest. Record your results in the table.
Write the number of sheets of tissue paper needed to stop the calculator display working.

Light source	Number of sheets of tissue paper
1	
2	
3	
4	
5	
6	

3 Write the light sources in order of brightness.

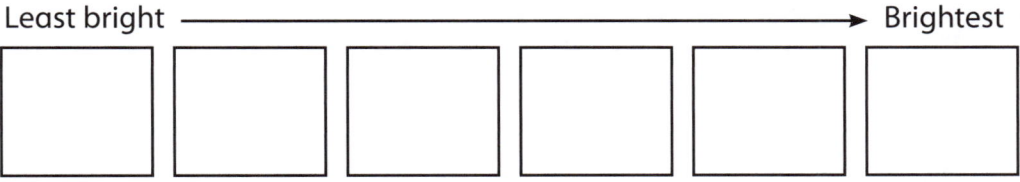

Least bright ⟶ Brightest

4 Was your prediction correct? **yes** **no**

Light intensity timeline

You are going to make a timeline of methods of measuring light intensity.

Here is an example of a timeline to help you.

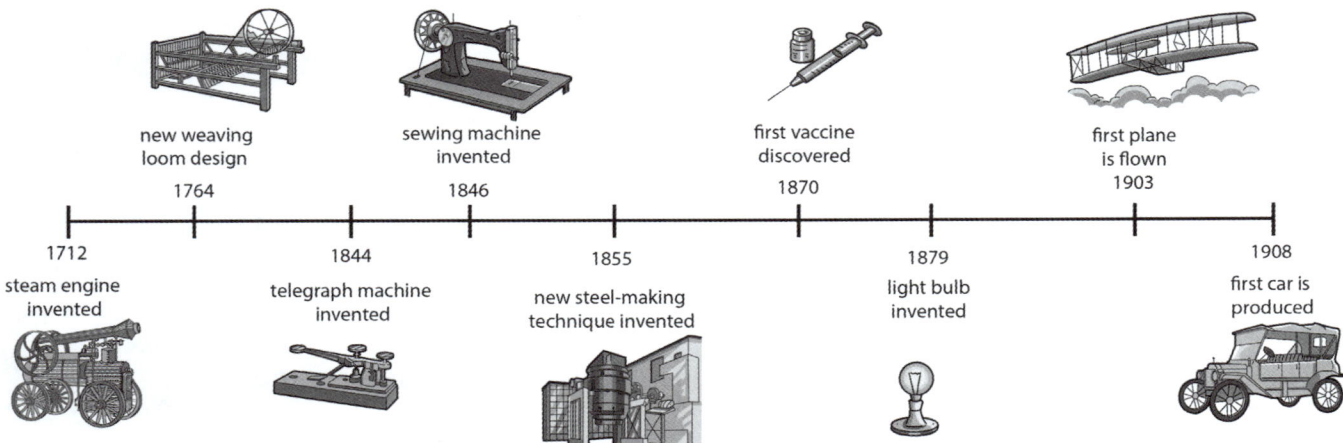

1   Work in a small research team. Use the internet or books for your research. You might find some information in your Student Book.

Here are some tips to help you:

- Find out the oldest methods. Start your timeline at this point.
- Include pictures and diagrams of the method. Add the date the method was found.
- What unit of measurement did they use?
- Find at least four methods used up to the current date.

2   Display your timeline in the school.

3   Compare your research with others. Did any of the other groups find a method that you did not?

Ask them to describe the method to you. Explain the method in the space below.

You can use diagrams and pictures to help you.

Distance and light intensity

Study the table below.

Distance from source (cm)	Light intensity (lux)
10	930
15	410
20	235
25	155
30	100
50	40
70	20
80	15
100	10

Distance and light intensity

1   Use the data to plot a line graph.

2   Decide how you will label the axes.

3   Make sure all the values fit within your graph. That means you will have to take one axis up to over 930!

4   What does your graph tell you about what happens to light intensity as the distance increases?

Stretch zone

Use your graph to determine the light intensity at a distance of 18 centimetres and 75 centimetres.

18 cm: _____

75 cm: _____

What I have learned about the way we see things

 What went well

1 Think about what you have learned.

2 Talk to a friend about something that went well in this unit.

3 Tick ✓ the boxes to rate yourself.

I can explore ways we use sight to learn about our world.	That's easy. ☐ That's challenging. ☐	Pages 70–75
I know that rays of light can be reflected by surfaces.	That's easy. ☐ That's challenging. ☐	Pages 76–79
I can explore why a beam of light changes direction when it is reflected.	That's easy. ☐ That's challenging. ☐	Pages 80–83
I know that we see colour because not all the light is reflected by some objects.	That's easy. ☐ That's challenging. ☐	Pages 84–85
I can explore how opaque materials block light and how transparent and translucent materials let light through.	That's easy. ☐ That's challenging. ☐	Pages 86–87
I know that shadows are formed when light travelling from a source is blocked.	That's easy. ☐ That's challenging. ☐	Pages 88–91
I can investigate how shadows change in length, size and position.	That's easy. ☐ That's challenging. ☐	Pages 92–97
I know that light intensity can be measured.	That's easy. ☐ That's challenging. ☐	Pages 98–101

 If you want to know more or need to check, go back to the pages in your Student Book.

Investigate like a scientist

Designing a model house of mirrors

Your design team is going to design a model of a house of mirrors.

1 Research the different mirrors used. Select three or four different designs to copy.

2 Make a model room out of an old box.

3 Copy the shape of the mirrors you have chosen. Use flexible or rolls of mirrors.

4 Attach the mirrors to your model.

5 Write a couple of sentences explaining how the mirrors work. Use a small toy.

6 Invite others to stand the toy in front of each mirror.

    a Did your design work?

    b Did people understand why the reflection was different?

Being an architect

You are going to design an outside shaded area for your school.

1 Determine when people will be outside. Make observations and measurements of the area during the day. Record these using a suitable method.

2 Design methods to keep the area in the shade when it is used.
To help you, consider these questions:

- Could you use any existing buildings or trees to give shade?
- Would you change the layout of the school?
- Would you move buildings, for example?
- Could you plant trees or shrubs in certain places?

Make a poster to show your designs. Fully explain your ideas.

4 Building Electrical Circuits

Key words

circuit

🔤 Read the word above out loud.

1 Write some words you know beginning with 'circ'.

2 Write your own definition for the word 'circuit'.

3 Compare your definition with the one your teacher gives you.

Did you define the word well? Do you need to change your definition at all?

Write your final definition here:

4 Draw a picture of a circuit to help you remember the meaning.

Introduction

Static electricity

 Can you make electricity with your hair or your clothes?

When you comb your hair, or rub a piece of plastic on your clothes, a small amount of electricity is made. The electricity does not move anywhere. We call it static electricity.

 How can you investigate this?

1 Try combing your hair, or rub a piece of plastic on your clothes. Then hold the comb or plastic near small pieces of paper. What happens to the pieces of paper?

2 Repeat Step 1, but this time move the comb or plastic over other small objects.

What can you see?

3 Electricity can also flow through wires.

Make a list of when you have used devices and appliances with wires.

4 Describe how you kept safe when using these devices and appliances.

Explain conductors and insulators

 Talk to someone else about all the insulators and conductors that you know about.

1 Design a leaflet to help younger children understand what conductors are and what insulators are.

- Draw pictures of conductors and insulators that the children might have seen.
- Explain what a conductor is and how it works.
- Describe which materials conductors are usually made from.
- Explain what an insulator is and how it works.
- Tell the children about the safety rules they must follow.

2 Write a list of conductors and insulators to help you remember them.

Conductors	Insulators

3 Complete the sentences to help you remember the important safety rules.

Never touch _____ wires.

Never touch sockets, plugs or electrical appliances with _____ hands.

Never put electrical appliances near _____.

Never put anything into an _____ _____.

Is it an insulator?

This activity supports the investigation on page 107 of your Student Book. You are going to investigate which materials are good insulators.

1 Set up a circuit using a battery, a bulb, wires and connectors. Leave two connectors free so that you can test materials. Use the diagram in the Student Book to help you.

2 Test your circuit to make sure everything is working.

3 Choose a material that you know is a good conductor. Write the name of this material.

_____

4 If everything is working, what will happen to the bulb?

_____

5 When your circuit is working, predict which materials will be a good insulator.

I predict that _____

_____.

6 Test the materials and record your findings in the table.

Material	Tick ✓ if it is an insulator

7 Which material would you use to insulate a wire?

_____

Choose your conductor

Research project: Ampère

Ampère was a scientist who is famous for making important discoveries about electricity.

Carry out a research project to find out about Ampère.

Present your findings on a poster or in an information leaflet.

You can use books, magazines, the internet or any other reliable source of information in your research.

Answer the questions to help you include all the important information.

André Marie Ampère.

1 What was Ampère's full name? _____

2 Where was he born? _____

3 When was he born? _____

4 What did he discover and invent?

_____

_____

5 Draw a picture of an invention made by Ampère.

6 What unit of measurement is named after him? _____

7 What does the unit measure? _____

8 What is the symbol for this unit? _____

Investigate the conductivity of metals

 This activity supports the investigations on page 109 of your Student Book.

Metals are very good conductors but some are better than others.

Which metal is the best conductor?

You are going to set up a test circuit and test six different metals.

1 Set up a test circuit using wires, connectors, a bulb and a battery.

2 Use a paperclip or a piece of metal to test that your circuit is working.

If the bulb does not light, change the components of the circuit one at a time until it is working.

3 Choose a piece of metal and write its name in the table.

4 Test the metal by joining the connectors to each side of the metal. Make sure they are properly connected or your results will not be reliable.

- If the bulb lights, the metal is a conductor.
- If the bulb is very bright, the metal is a good conductor.

5 Record your results in the first and second columns in the table.

Metal	How bright is the bulb?	Order of the best to worst conductors

6 Now number the metals in order of conductivity, from the best conductor (1) to the worst conductor (6). Write the number in the third column of the table.

The metal that makes the bulb shine brightest is the best conductor so it will be number 1.

Wiring a plug

1 Look at the diagram of the plug. Label the parts.

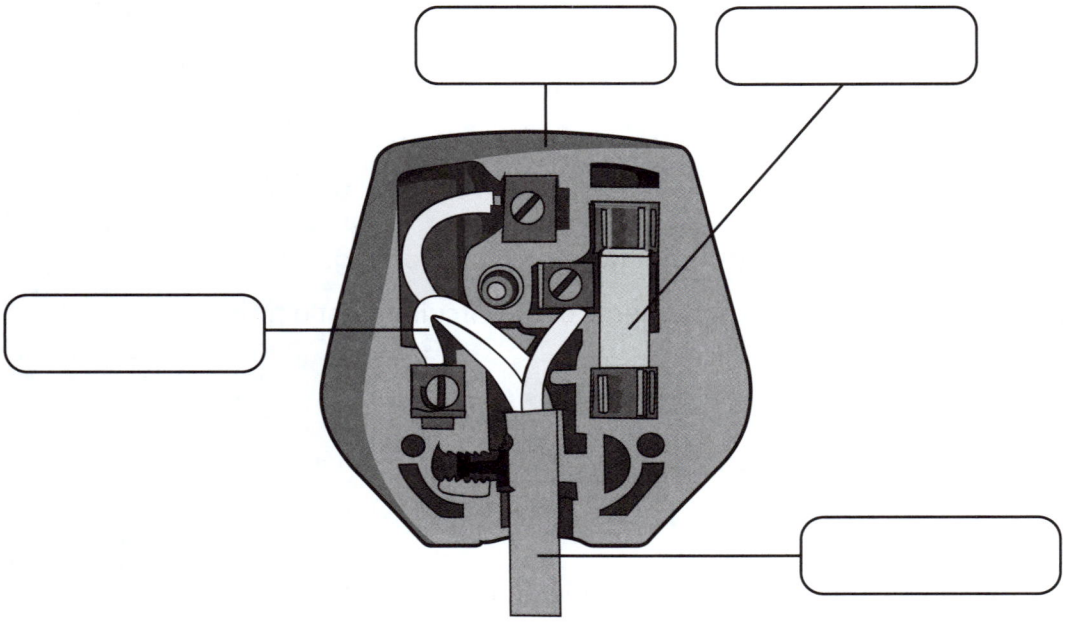

2 What colour are the different wires? Colour the wires in the correct colours.

3 What are the different parts of the plug made from? Label each part C for conductor or I for insulator.

4 Choose two parts of the plug and state what each part does. Complete the table.

Part of the plug	What it does

What have you learned so far?

1 Explain why an electrical circuit is called a circuit.

2 Can you list any materials from your investigations that will make good insulators?

3 Why is it important to turn off the computer before anyone tries to mend the wire?

4 Name a metal that is a good conductor.

5 What materials, other than metals, can conduct electricity?

6 Why are wires covered in plastic?

7 What metal is used in wires around the house? Why is it used?

8 Explain why aluminium is used in overhead cables.

Changing circuits

Changing the components in a circuit

 This activity supports the investigations on pages 112–113 of your Student Book. What happens when we change parts of a circuit?

1 Draw a circuit diagram of the circuit you will use for this investigation.

2 Decide the changes you will make.

> **Remember:** You can only change one thing at a time. Everything else in the circuit must stay the same. Otherwise, it will not be a fair test and you will not be able to compare your results.

3 Predict what you think will happen to your circuit when you make each change.

4 Carry out each change.

5 Observe what happens to the circuit.

Use the table to record your predictions and results. An example has been done for you.

Change made	Predict what will happen	What happened?
Add one bulb	The bulbs will be brighter	None of the bulbs lit up

6 Look at your results.

- Did any of the results surprise you?
- Were any of your predictions wrong?

Investigating the thickness of a wire

 You are going to use some wires of different thicknesses to test the effect on the brightness of the bulb in a circuit.

The wires may be labelled with a measurement of their thickness. The thickness of a wire is called the gauge.

1 Order the wires according to how thick they look.

2 Predict which wire will make the bulb light the brightest.

3 Design an investigation to test and record your results.

You could take a photograph of the set up and stick it in the space below or draw a diagram.

4 Why is it important to show people exactly how you carried out an investigation?

5 Record your results in the table.

Thickness of wire	Predict what will happen	Observation

6 Conclusion: Does the thickness of the wire affect how bright the bulb lights up?

Circuit breakers

How does a filament bulb work?

You are going to find out about filament bulbs.

1 Draw a diagram of an old-fashioned filament bulb.

2 Explain how the bulb gives out light.

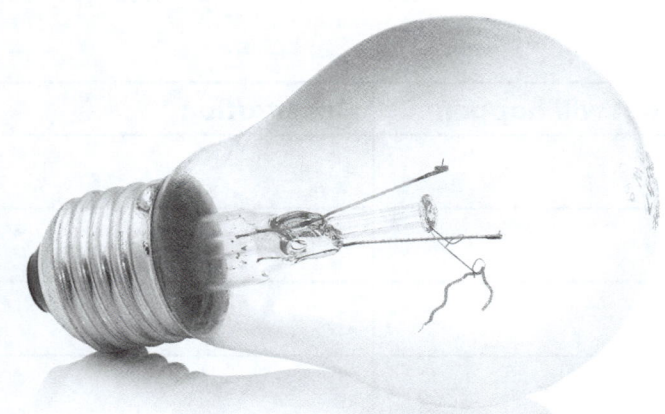

 **3** Look at the photograph. Explain what could have happened to this bulb.

Why will it not give out light when it is connected to an electrical supply?

Does the width of a wire affect how hot it gets?

This activity supports the investigation on page 115 of your Student Book.

1 Explain what a circuit breaker is.

2 Draw a diagram of a fuse. Explain how the fuse acts as a safety device in a circuit.

3 Can you see if the wire is beginning to get hot? Is it glowing?

Record your results from your investigation in the table.

Width of wire	Is the wire glowing?

4 Conclusion: Does the width of the wire affect how hot it gets?

Using circuit diagrams

Answer the following questions for each circuit diagram below.

1 Will this circuit light the bulb?

2 If not, what will you need to change to make the bulb light?

3 Will the bulb light brightly or dimly? Explain your answer.

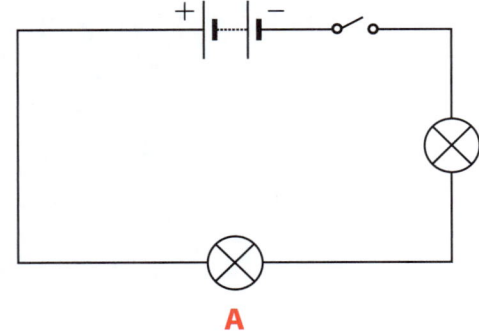

A

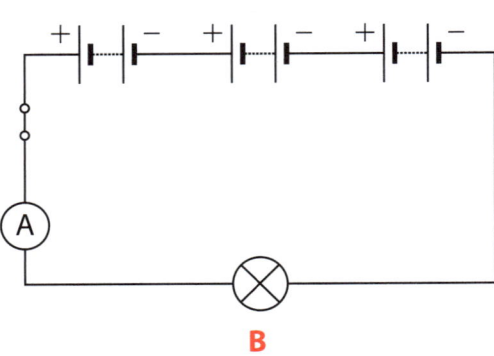

B

1 _____

2 _____

3 _____

1 _____

2 _____

3 _____

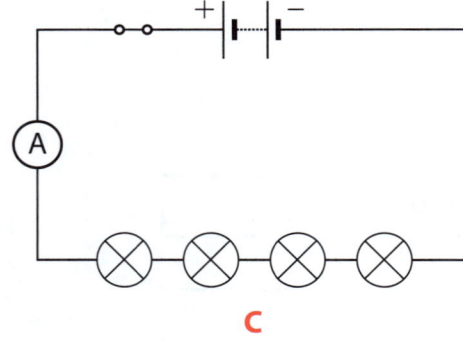

C

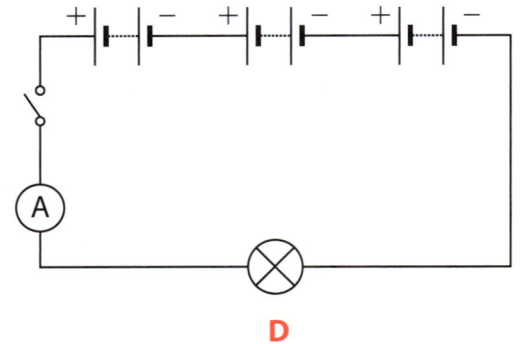

D

1 _____

2 _____

3 _____

1 _____

2 _____

3 _____

Drawing circuits

1 Draw the following circuit diagrams. Include all of the components listed.

Circle the correct answer to state whether or not each circuit will work.

a Two batteries, a buzzer and a closed switch.

This circuit   **will / will not**   work.

b A closed switch, two batteries, three bulbs and a buzzer.

This circuit   **will / will not**   work.

c An ammeter, an open switch, a battery and a motor.

This circuit   **will / will not**   work.

2 For your circuit in question 1c, will there be a reading on the ammeter? Explain your answer.

Build circuits from diagrams and test them

Which circuits light the bulbs?

Look at the circuit diagrams.

Remember: There might not be enough energy. You may have to add batteries or remove something from the circuit.

1   Build the circuits shown in the diagrams to test whether or not they light the bulb (or bulbs).

2   If a circuit doesn't light the bulbs, try to find out why. Try to adapt the circuit to make the bulbs light.

Under each circuit diagram write down what you changed and how bright the bulbs are.

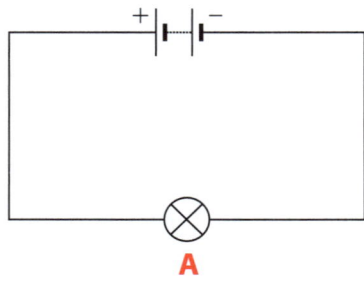

A

_____

_____

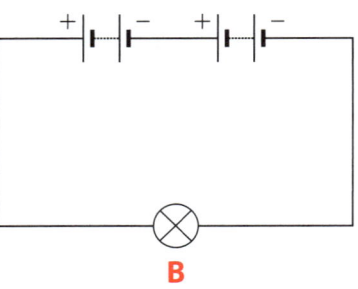

B

_____

_____

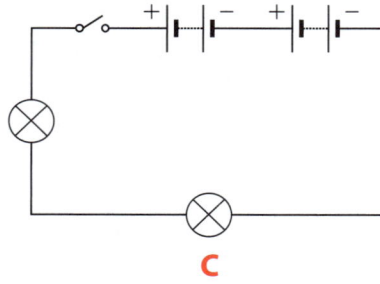

C

_____

_____

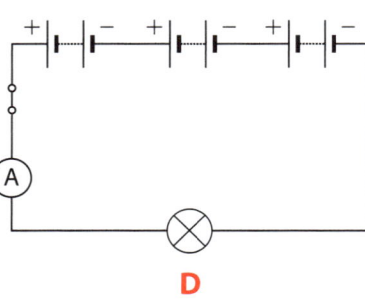

D

_____

_____

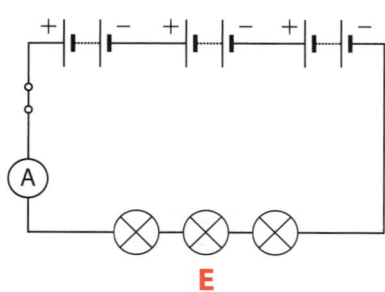

E

_____

_____

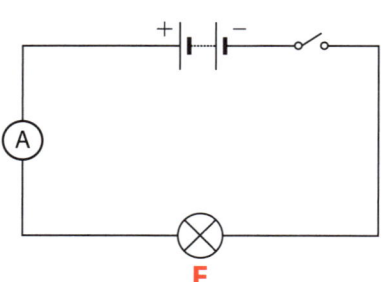

F

_____

_____

Investigating series and parallel circuits

This activity supports the investigation on page 119 of your Student Book.

Look at the circuit diagrams below.

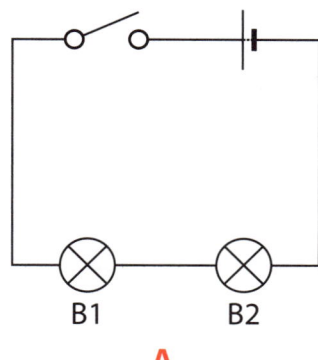

A

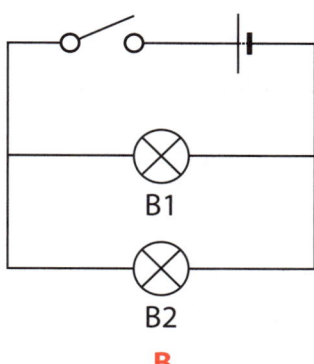

B

1 Write down one difference between the two circuits.

2 Which circuit shows a parallel circuit? _____

3 Set up the circuits. Write in your prediction:

Before I close the switches, I predict that circuit _____ will have the brightest bulbs.

4 Close the switches. Compare the brightness of the bulbs. Record your observations.

The bulbs in Circuit A are _____ than the bulbs in Circuit B.

Was your prediction correct?   **yes**   **no**

5 Remove bulb B2 from each circuit. Predict what will happen to the other bulbs.

In Circuit A, bulb B1 will _____. This is because _____.

In Circuit B, bulb B1 will _____. This is because _____.

6 Record your observations.

Were your predictions correct?   **yes**   **no**

Stretch zone

Produce a short information sheet to tell people about series and parallel circuits.

Measuring voltage

Using a voltmeter

 This activity supports the investigation on page 121 of your Student Book.

1 Set up the three circuits shown below.

Start with Circuit A.

You will need a voltmeter. Look carefully at how it connects in each circuit.

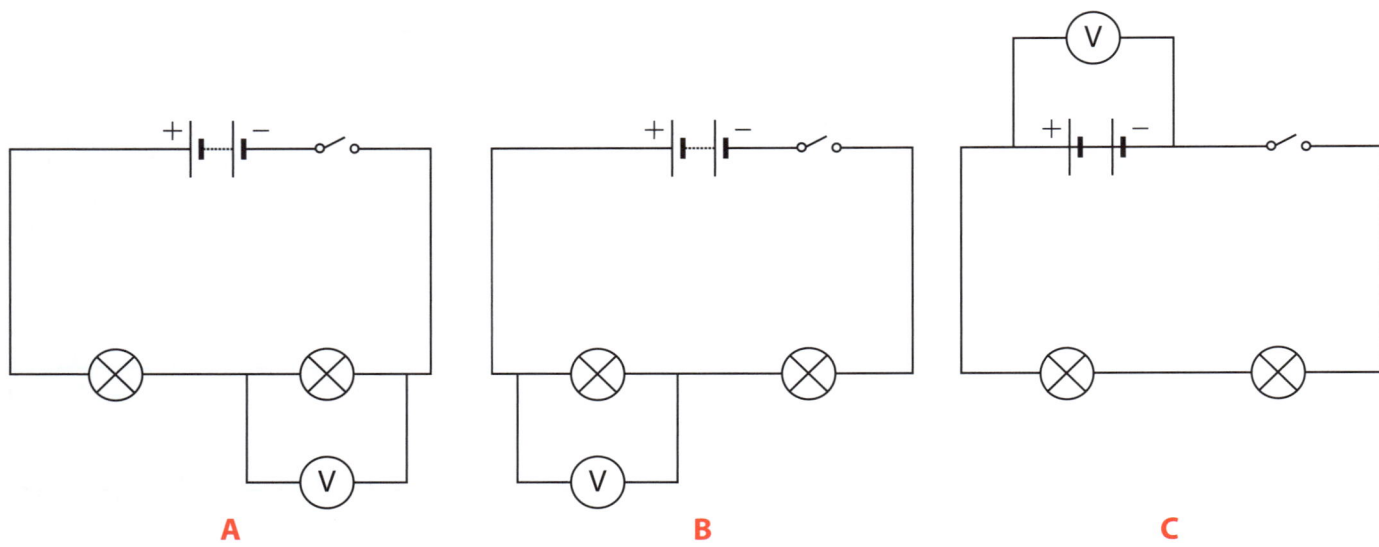

A   B   C

2 Read the number of volts on the voltmeter for each circuit.

3 Record this in the table below.

Circuit	Number of volts
A	
B	
C	

4 Compare the readings. Are all the readings the same?

5 Does the position of the voltmeter change the reading?

Making a battery

You will need: seven copper coins, aluminium foil, thin card, lemon juice or vinegar, salt, paper towel, sticky tape, an LED and wires, a voltmeter.

1   Put the coins in a dish. Add some lemon juice or vinegar and salt to clean them. Blot them dry with a paper towel.

2   Cut the aluminium foil and the card into circles the same size as the coins. Soak the card in lemon juice or vinegar.

3   Build a tower of coins: start with a coin, then add a circle of soaked card and then a circle of aluminium. Then add another coin, and so on. This will make a voltaic pile or battery.

4   Stick one wire to the bottom of the pile and another wire to the top. Hold them in place using the tape. Then, wrap the pile in tape to keep it all together.

5   What happens when you connect a voltmeter or an LED to the wires?

Using circuit diagrams to make predictions

Model circuits

You are going to make models of circuits. Use string and paper plates or card to make models of the circuits shown in the diagrams.

You will need: paper plates or pieces of card, a ball of string, scissors, sticky tape.

1 Draw the symbol for each component on a paper plate or piece of card (one symbol on each).

2 The string represents the wires. Cut lengths of string and stick them between the paper plates or card.

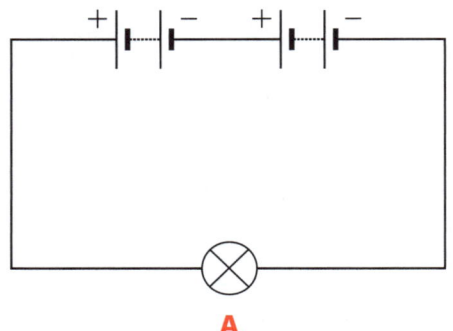

A

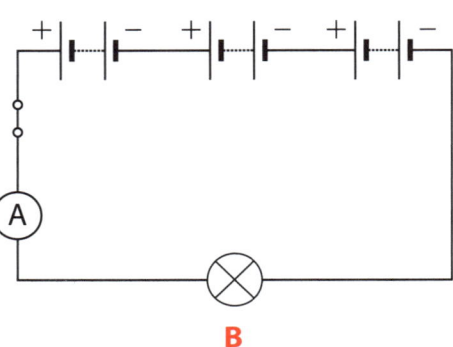

B

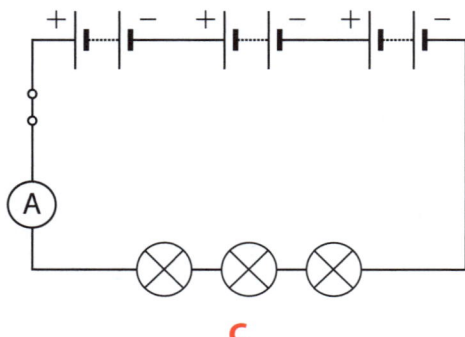

C

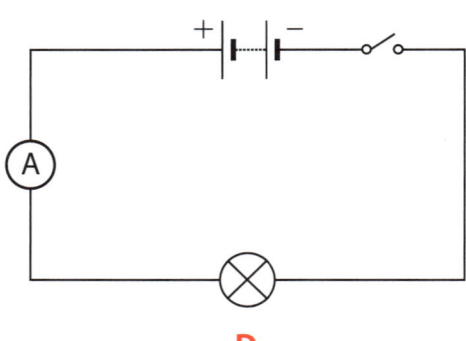

D

3 Display your models in school. Ask a classmate to draw the circuit diagrams shown in your models.

Circuit wordsearch

 1 Find some words from this unit in the wordsearch.

Circle each word in the grid when you find it. One example has been done for you.

e	s	d	x	p	l	a	s	t	i	c
b	k	w	n	d	w	t	v	q	c	s
a	u	d	i	u	s	y	m	b	o	l
t	j	z	s	t	f	v	l	z	n	m
t	b	y	z	r	c	g	q	z	d	d
e	z	u	b	e	i	h	m	x	u	i
r	m	o	l	t	r	s	e	r	c	a
y	w	p	v	b	c	h	t	i	t	g
t	c	i	n	s	u	l	a	t	o	r
q	w	b	r	z	i	a	l	j	r	a
u	a	m	m	e	t	e	r	v	k	m

> **ammeter   battery   bulb   buzzer   ~~circuit diagram~~**
> **conductor   insulator   metal   plastic   switch   symbol   wire**

2 Explain to a partner what each word means.

3 Draw the symbol for each of these components.

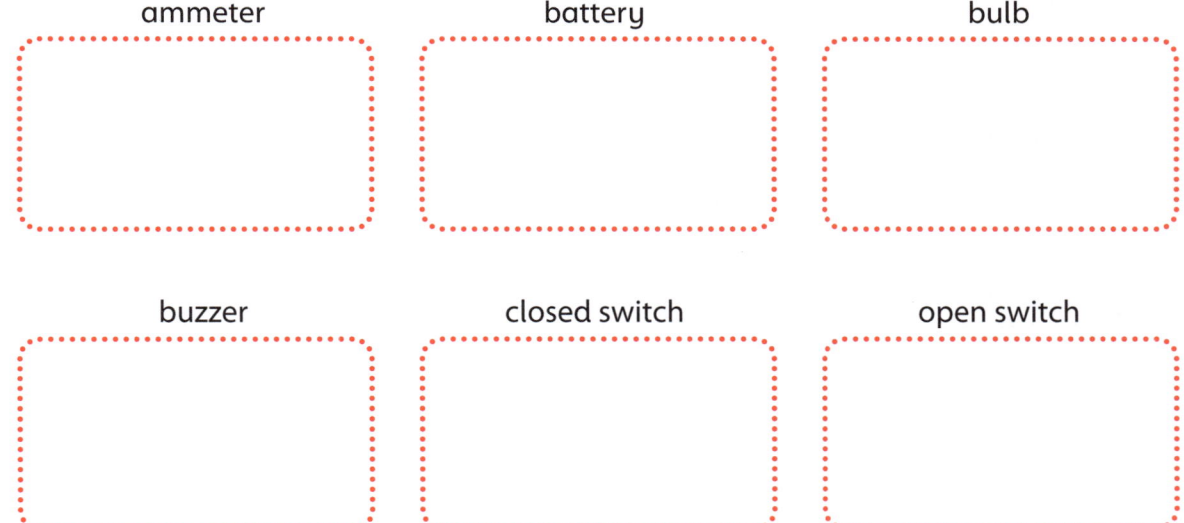

ammeter

battery

bulb

buzzer

closed switch

open switch

4 Building Electrical Circuits

What I have learned about building electrical circuits

 What went well

1 Think about what you have learned.

2 Talk to a friend about something that went well in this unit.

3 Tick ✓ the boxes to rate yourself.

I can investigate how some materials are better conductors of electricity than others.	That's easy. ☐ That's challenging. ☐	Pages 106–109
I know why metals are used for cables and wires, and why plastics are used to cover wires or for plug and switch covers.	That's easy. ☐ That's challenging. ☐	Pages 110–111
I can predict and test the effects of making changes to circuits.	That's easy. ☐ That's challenging. ☐	Pages 112–115 and 122–123
I can represent series circuits with drawings and conventional symbols.	That's easy. ☐ That's challenging. ☐	Pages 116–121

☺ If you want to know more or need to check, go back to the pages in your Student Book.

Investigate like a scientist

Can a pencil be used to complete a circuit?

You have made circuits and tested materials to find out if they are insulators or conductors of electricity.

Imagine you are part of a team of electricians and engineers. One of the circuits in a school has stopped working. You and your team find that there is a break in a wire, but you don't have any wires to replace it.

1   The school has been wired using series circuits. Why do you need to repair this one quickly? Describe the situation in the school during the breakage.

2   Someone suggests using a pencil in place of the wire. Do you predict that this will work?

3   Design an investigation to test this.

4   Research the properties of the pencil.

5   Carry out your investigation. Do your research findings support the results of your test?

6   Present your investigation and findings as a news report.

   Can the pencil be used to fix the problem?

Making symbols

You are going to invent new symbols for circuit components.

1   Find 20 symbols for components that you recognise or have heard of. Use the internet or books to help you.

2   Design new symbols for these components.

> **Remember:** Why do we use symbols instead of drawings? Make your symbols work in the same way. You could change them so that they make more sense to younger people.

3   Present your new symbols as a booklet.

   Include the name of the symbol, the old symbol, your new symbol and a brief description of what the component does.

5 Adaptation and Inherited Characteristics

Key words

1 Find some of the key words in this unit hidden below.

Circle each one as you find it.

e	h	w	e	u	c	u	n	s	b	c	l	a	w
l	h	o	l	h	q	g	a	n	h	w	o	t	s
v	s	v	a	r	i	a	t	i	o	n	t	b	g
a	d	a	p	t	a	t	i	o	n	w	q	n	a
k	f	i	y	f	o	e	g	m	y	d	r	w	m
i	r	o	p	w	v	q	p	t	c	e	a	v	y
r	y	t	c	u	d	q	u	f	o	s	s	i	l
e	x	t	i	n	c	t	v	h	i	x	z	h	b
r	e	p	r	o	d	u	c	t	i	o	n	u	b
a	n	c	e	s	t	o	r	k	v	n	s	c	r
u	d	x	f	b	u	x	w	e	u	x	i	g	v
q	n	q	z	s	l	w	s	p	e	c	i	e	s
p	f	w	o	f	f	s	p	r	i	n	g	q	p
a	i	n	h	e	r	i	t	b	r	t	c	s	a

2 Write down any key words below that you have not used before. Tick ✓ them when you have learned about them later in this unit.

Introduction

Match the definition

Draw a line to join each key word with its definition.

adaptation	Evidence of living things preserved in rocks.
ancestor	The making of new individuals by parents.
extinct	The differences between individuals in a species.
fossil	The young born to living things.
inherit	The passing of characteristics from parents to their offspring.
offspring	The living things that other living things developed from.
reproduction	Living things that are so similar they can make offspring together.
species	Any characteristic that helps a living thing survive in its habitat.
variation	A species that no longer exists.

The fossil record

How are fossils formed?

Place the pictures into the correct order. Write the letters in the sequence boxes at the bottom of the page.

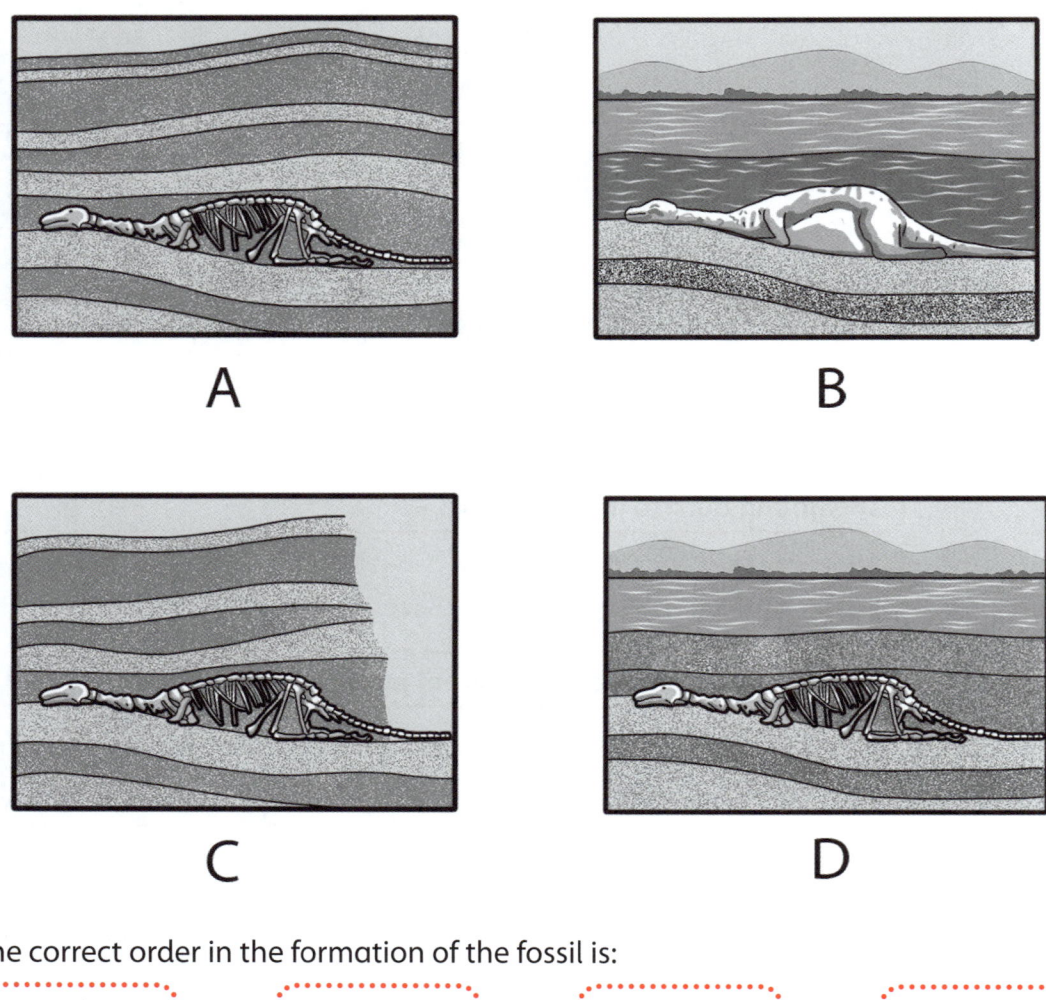

A

B

C

D

The correct order in the formation of the fossil is:

☐ → ☐ → ☐ → ☐

Hint: Look at the animal. Can you see its body or is it a skeleton?

Is it on the sea bed or is it buried?

How many layers is it buried under?

Have the layers started to be worn away to show the skeleton?

Making a plaster cast fossil model

 This activity supports the investigation on page 128 of your Student Book.

Choose an example of a once-living thing. This can be a seashell or parts of a plant.

1 Roll a ball of clay into a disc that is 15 centimetres in diameter and 2 centimetres thick.

2 Fold up the edges of the disc so it makes a shallow dish.

3 Press your once-living thing into the flat surface of the clay.

4 Remove the once-living thing. It will leave a mould.

5 Add 5 cm³ of water to 12 grams of plaster of Paris. Stir the mixture.

6 Pour the plaster of Paris into your dish and leave it to set for one hour.

Warning! Do not get plaster of Paris onto your skin or into your eyes. What could happen if you did?

7 Carefully remove the plaster of Paris from your dish and leave it to dry overnight.

8 Paint your fossil and display it with a clear label explaining what it is.

9 Move around the displays. Try to identify the fossils.

Changes over time

Handling data about change

This activity supports the investigation on page 131 of your Student Book.

Study the data below. It shows the average height of modern horses and their ancestors. It also shows when they lived.

Animal	Height in meters	Date the animals lived (millions of years ago)
A	0.4	45–55
B	0.6	30–40
C	1.0	15–25
D	1.25	5–15
E	1.6	present time–5

1 Which letter represents the modern horse? _____

2 Which ancestor of the modern horse is the smallest? _____

3 How tall was the ancestor of the horse that lived 16 million years ago? _____

4 Present the data as a chart. Use the axes below. Remember to label each bar with the letter of the animal.

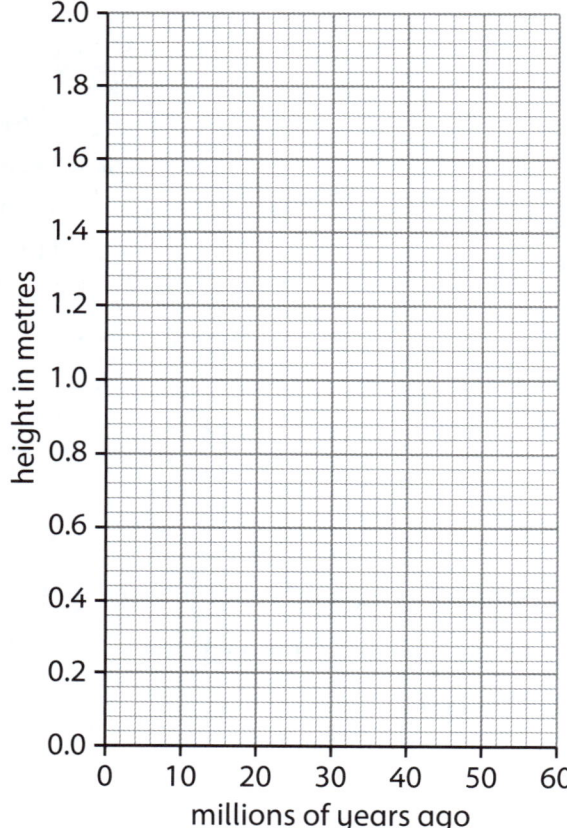

Changes in plants

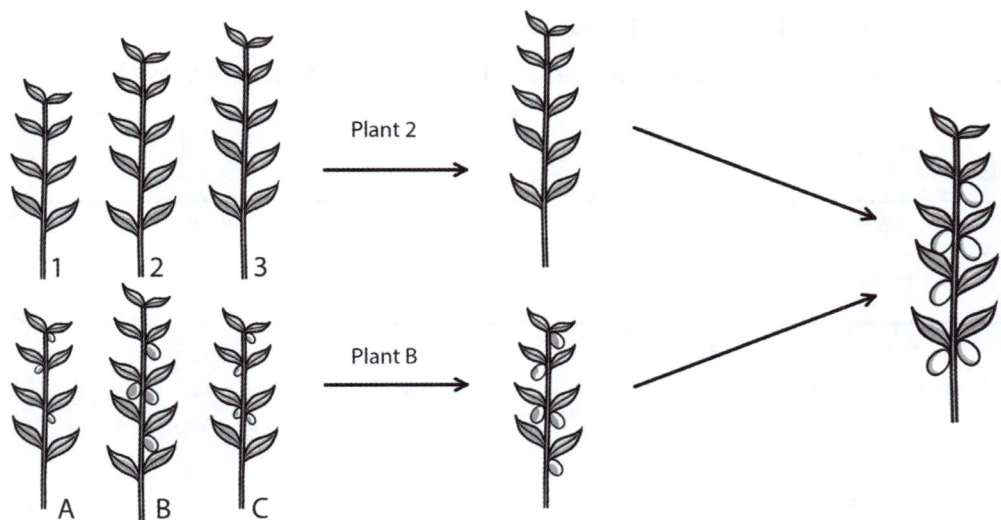

Scientists and farmers have been helping animals and plants to change by deliberately mixing up characteristics that are useful to people. They mix characteristics from different varieties of plants by adding pollen from one plant to the stigma of another. This is called crossing.

1 Look at the diagram above. Why would a scientist select plants 2 and B in this investigation?

2 In the boxes below, draw your prediction of what the plants would look like if the following plant characteristics were crossed.

   a Plants 1 and A

   b Plants 2 and A

Plants 1 and A

Plants 2 and A

5 Adaptation and Inherited Characteristics

Offspring inherit characteristics

Seed investigation

This activity supports the investigation on page 133 of your Student Book.

Collect your four different types of unlabelled seeds. Your teacher will show you the plants they could have come from.

1 How are the seeds different?

2 Predict which plant each seed has come from.

A is from _____. B is from _____.

C is from _____. D is from _____.

3 Take four pots and label them A, B, C and D.

Add the same amount of compost to each one.

4 Plant five seeds in each pot. Remember to put seeds A into pot A!

Water the seeds and leave them in a warm, dark place.

Keep the compost moist and observe your seeds until they germinate.

5 Move the seedlings to a warm, sunny place as soon as they appear.

Observe the plants and keep comparing them to the possible parent plants.

6 Record your findings in the table below.

Seeds	Date planted	Date seedlings appear	Which adult plant do they look like?
A			
B			
C			
D			

7 a Were your predictions correct?   **yes**   **no**   **some**

    b Did the plants produce offspring like the parent plant?   **yes**   **no**   **some**

8 Now produce a short computer or poster presentation to describe your investigation and your findings.

Find the parent

1 Draw lines to match each young living thing with its most likely parent.

2 An animal offspring that looks like the adult is _____.

3 An animal offspring that does not look like the adult is _____.

4 Two things that adult plants might have that their offspring will not have are

_____ and _____.

Investigating variation in hand size

This activity builds on the investigation on page 135 of your Student Book.
You are going to investigate hand span instead of shoe size.

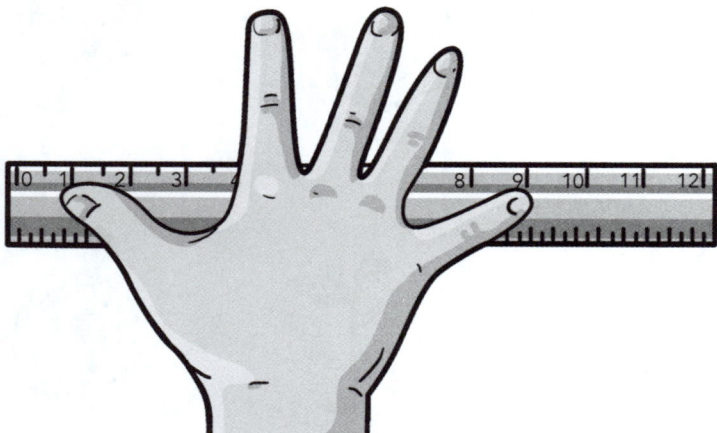

1 Plan your investigation.

2 Survey eight people in your class.

3 Record the results in the table below.

Hand span (in centimetres)	Number of people with this hand span

4 Produce a bar chart or a line graph to show the results.

5 What is the average hand span for the people you surveyed? _____

6 How much variation in hand span did you notice? _____

Investigating variation in plants

This activity supports the investigation on page 135 of your Student Book.

You are going to collect some seeds from a plant in your area.

Warning! Check with an adult before taking any seeds from plants. Why is this important?

1 Plant five seeds 1 centimetre apart in a large pot of compost or in the soil.

   Label the seeds A, B, C, D and E.

   Water the seeds and leave them in a warm, dark place.

2 Observe your seeds every day and keep the compost moist but not wet.

3 When you see seedlings move your pot to a warm, sunny place.

> **Remember:** Carry out a fair test and bear in mind environmental factors such as light and water.

4 Observe and measure your seedlings on the days shown in the table.

   Record your results in the table.

Seedling	Height in centimetres				
	Day 1	Day 3	Day 7	Day 10	Day 14
A					
B					
C					
D					
E					

5 Interpret your table. Was there any variation in the offspring produced by the seeds?

Adapting to the environment

Adaptations for feeding

You are going to think about how birds' beaks are adapted for feeding.

Draw lines to link the bird to the type of food you think it is most likely to eat, based on the shape of its beak.

nuts

small seeds

small animals

insects buried in mud

insects in bark

small fish

nectar

Stretch zone

Research a bird called a pelican.

a Draw a pelican below and write down how its beak is adapted to help it feed.

b The pelican's beak is adapted by _____

_____

Plant adaptation survey

 This activity supports the investigation on page 137 of your Student Book.
You are going to survey different plants and make a presentation.

1   Use the checklist below to help you identify plant adaptations. Tick ✓ any
    you find.

> **Warning!** You may not find all these plants in your area.
> Some plants are adapted to live in different habitats – such as
> water, rainforest, desert, cold areas and grassland.

Checklist:

- ☐ spines, stingers or spikes on the plant to stop it from being eaten
- ☐ wide roots to help in collecting water over a wide area
- ☐ deep roots to search into soil for water
- ☐ large leaves to help in making food, using energy from the Sun
- ☐ grows towards the light
- ☐ grows tall to obtain more light
- ☐ tendrils to help them to climb other plants
- ☐ large flowers to attract insects
- ☐ scented flowers to attract insects
- ☐ small leaves or spines to prevent drying out
- ☐ waxy leaves to prevent loss of water
- ☐ thick bark to prevent drying out
- ☐ strong stems or trunks to grow tall
- ☐ smooth bark to prevent other plants climbing up

2   Scientists use many different ways of recording their observations.

    Photograph or film your examples of plant adaptations. These can go in
    your presentation.

Adaptation trail

This activity supports the investigation on page 139 of your Student Book.

You are going to set out an adaptation trail.

1 Take some pieces of coloured card and cut out 15 identical insect shapes.

Five should be blue, five should be green and five should be red. This is your population.

2 Place your insect shapes on plants around the school.

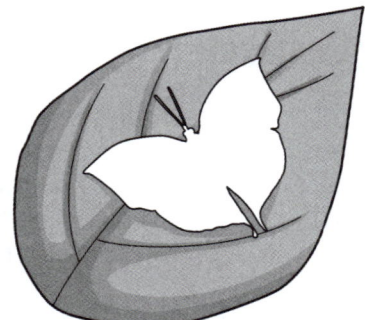

3 Ask someone to look for your insects for five minutes and fill in the table below.

Colour of insect	Number found after five minutes
red	
green	
blue	

4 Which insect was most easily seen? _____

5 Which insect was the hardest to see? Why? _____

_____

6 Which insect would survive to make offspring? _____

_____

Capture release data

Doctor Henry Kettlewell studied peppered moths to investigate adaptation and change. He caught some moths, counted them, and put a small paint mark under their wings. He then released them. For the next few nights he investigated how many he could recapture. He did this in a polluted forest where the trees would be dirty and dark. He also did this in an unpolluted forest, where the trees would be cleaner and lighter in colour.

His results are below.

Polluted forest			Unpolluted forest		
	pale moth	**dark moth**		**pale moth**	**dark moth**
number released	201	601	number released	496	473
number recaptured	34	205	number recaptured	62	30
% recaptured	16	34	% recaptured	12	6

1 Which variety of moth was recaptured most often in the polluted forest?

> **pale**   **dark**

2 What could have happened to the other variety of moth?

3 Which variety of moth was recaptured most often in the unpolluted forest?

> **pale**   **dark**

4 What could have happened to the other variety of moth?

5 What do Doctor Kettlewell's results tell us about adaptation and survival?

What I have learned about adaptation and inherited characteristics

What went well

1   Think about what you have learned.

2   Talk to a friend about something that went well in this unit.

3   Tick ✓ the boxes to rate yourself.

I know that living things have changed over time and fossils provide a record of this.	That's easy. ☐ That's challenging. ☐	Pages 128–129
I know that living things produce offspring but these offspring usually vary from their parents.	That's easy. ☐ That's challenging. ☐	Pages 130–131
I know that living things adapt to suit their environment and that adaptation can lead to eventual changes in species.	That's easy. ☐ That's challenging. ☐	Pages 132–139

 If you want to know more or need to check, go back to the pages in your Student Book.

Investigate like a scientist

Investigating beak adaptations

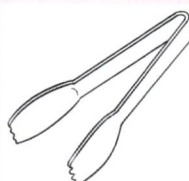 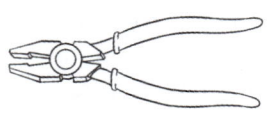 

These tools will be your model beaks

You will need: a plate or shallow dish with water in, a large bowl of water, pebbles, a piece of wood with small holes in, small seeds, rice, a dry dish, pieces of cork or polystyrene, tweezers, pliers, salad tongs, a stop watch or timer.

1 Take it in turns to use one of the model beaks to pick up as many pieces of food from each area as you can in 30 seconds. Once you have picked up the food put it into a cup.

The foods will be found in:

- marsh – a plate of water with floating objects such as cork or polystyrene
- pond – a large bowl of water with pebbles at the bottom
- forest – the piece of wood with holes in filled with small seeds
- grassland – a dry dish with dry rice in the bottom.

Warning! You must not touch the food or water with your hands. Do not pick up food from the table.

2 Record your results in the table.

Area	Number of pieces of food collected by each beak type		
	tweezers	salad tongs	pliers
marsh			
pond			
forest			
grassland			

3 What do your results tell you about beak adaptations and obtaining food?

5 Adaptation and Inherited Characteristics

How to use these questions

These quiz questions and activities are intended to encourage students to reflect on their learning and to reinforce their developing knowledge about scientific concepts in a fun way. They are flexible enough to be individual, pair or group activities. The questions can be used in a number of ways:

- Questions can be selected from this section to supplement work carried out during each module, to act as extra tasks and support for individuals, groups and whole classes. In this way, they can aid differentiation.
- Students can tackle the relevant questions at the end of each module to review learning and supplement the 'What I have learned' sections.
- Students can undertake questions at the end of a series of modules or even at the end of the year to review learning. The questions could be set in batches over a series of lessons or even taken as a small timed test – although this is not their main purpose.

① Classification and Habitats

1 Solve the clues about the environment to complete the crossword.

Across

3 Reuse waste by making it into new products.

5 Protection of the environment and living things.

6 The process caused by the atmosphere trapping the Sun's heat energy (two words).

8 All the things that we no longer need and throw away.

9 Rainfall that is polluted and can damage living and non-living things (two words).

11 A method of waste disposal that involves burying the waste.

12 The natural world where we live.

Down

1 The process of cutting down trees on a very large scale.

2 Harmful substances mixing with the water, air or soil.

4 Waste that is thrown away carelessly on the ground.

7 The place where an animal or plant lives.

10 To look after. We must do this for the environment.

2 a Use the key to identify the two animals. Write the names in the boxes.

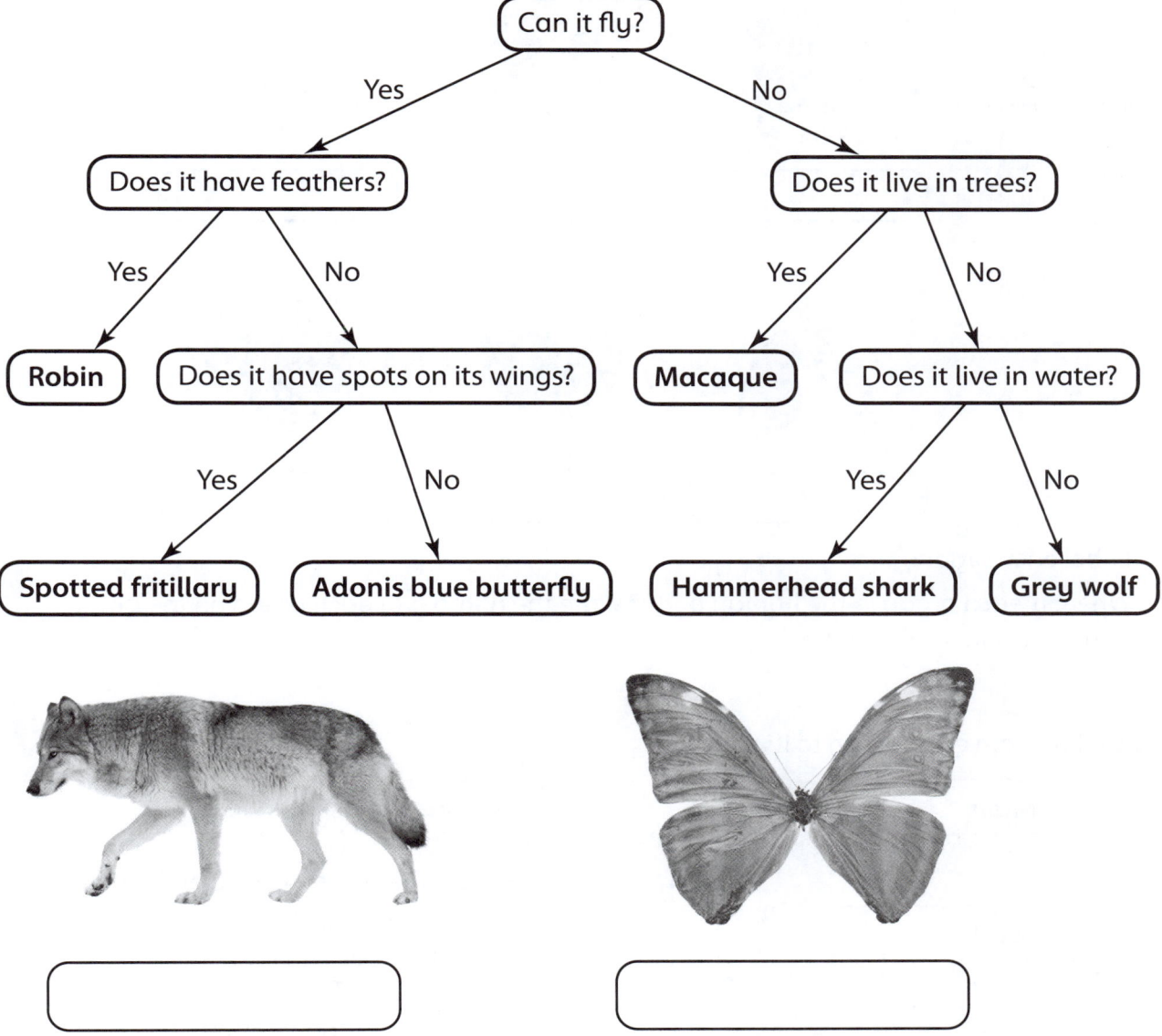

Can it fly?

Yes → Does it have feathers?

No → Does it live in trees?

Does it have feathers?
Yes → Robin
No → Does it have spots on its wings?

Does it live in trees?
Yes → Macaque
No → Does it live in water?

Does it have spots on its wings?
Yes → Spotted fritillary
No → Adonis blue butterfly

Does it live in water?
Yes → Hammerhead shark
No → Grey wolf

b The hammerhead shark is a vertebrate and is classified into the class called fish. List the other four vertebrate classes.

_____   _____

_____   _____

2 Organs and Systems

3 Look at the organs of the human body.

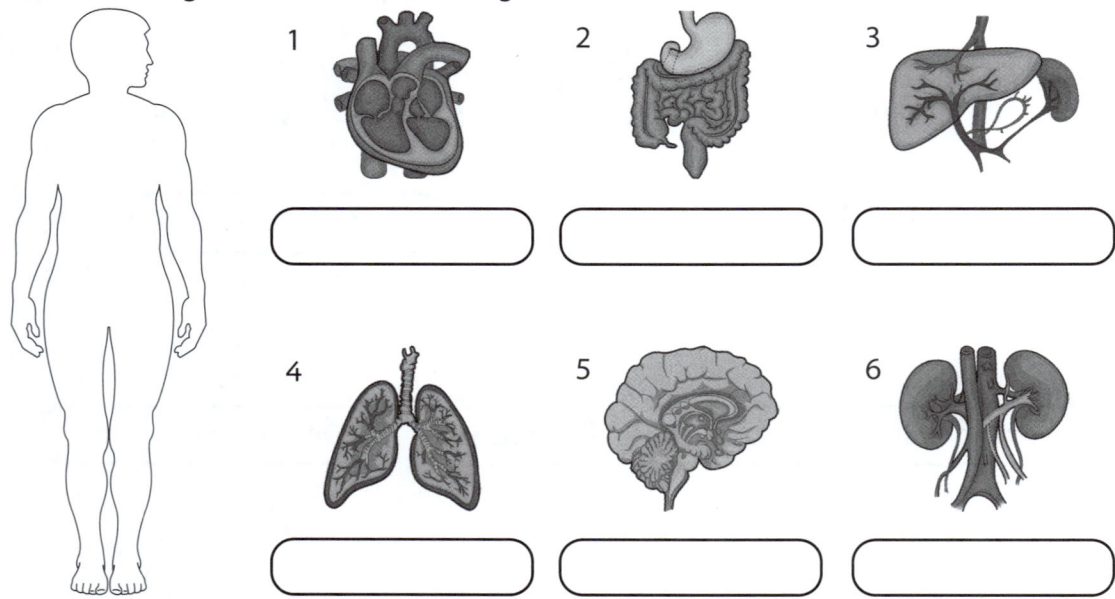

a Label each organ.

b Where is each organ in the human body? Write the number of each organ on the body outline to show where it belongs.

4 Draw a line from each organ to its function.

brain	We breathe air into these.
heart	This is the control centre of the body. It does millions of tasks without you thinking about them.
lungs	This pumps blood around the body in tubes called blood vessels.
stomach and intestines	This removes harmful chemicals from the blood. It also produces bile to help us digest our food.
kidneys	Food is digested and absorbed here.
liver	We have two of these. They filter the blood and remove urea and ammonia, which are excreted in urine.

❸ The Way We See Things

5 Complete the ray diagram. Draw a line to show the path of a beam of light leaving the torch.

6 Look at the shadow. The person is standing in front of a lamp and the lamp is casting their shadow onto a wall.

a What will the shadow look like if the person moves closer to the lamp? Draw this shadow in Box A.

b What will the shadow look like if the person moves nearer to the wall? Draw this shadow in Box B.

A

B

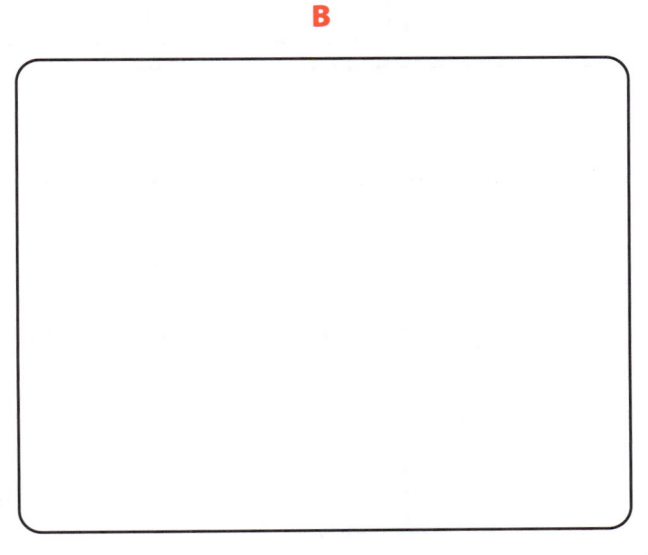

4 Building Electrical Circuits

7 Look at the pictures of some components for electrical circuits.
Draw the circuit symbol of each component in the box below it.

8 a Complete the diagram. Use the words in the box. Order these from the worst
to the best conductor.

> aluminium
> copper
> gold
> graphite
> mercury

Conductivity

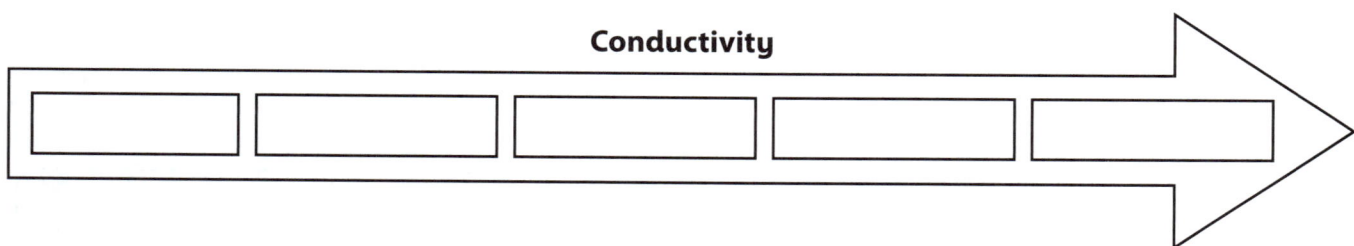

b Which metal is used in homes to carry electrical charge in wires?

_____

c Which metal is used for cables that carry electrical charge from the power plant to homes?

_____

d Give one reason why we don't use the metal that is the best conductor for this purpose.

9 a Unscramble the anagrams and write the key words for Unit 4 in the boxes.

b Write a definition for each word.

ciciutr 　☐☐☐☐☐☐☐

Definition: _____

rsnuitalo 　☐☐☐☐☐☐☐☐☐

Definition: _____

dncotrocu 　☐☐☐☐☐☐☐☐☐

Definition: _____

trbytae 　☐☐☐☐☐☐☐

Definition: _____

⑤ Adaptation and Inherited Characteristics

10 Complete the crossword.

Across

4 The differences between individuals in a species.

6 Young born to living things.

9 The process where living things acquire characteristics from their parents.

Down

1 Living things that are so similar they can produce offspring together.

2 Living things from long ago that other living things have developed from.

3 The process where living things make new individuals.

5 Characteristics that help living things to survive in their habitats.

7 Evidence of once-living things preserved in rocks.

8 The dying out of a species.

11   Look at the diagram about breeding plants.

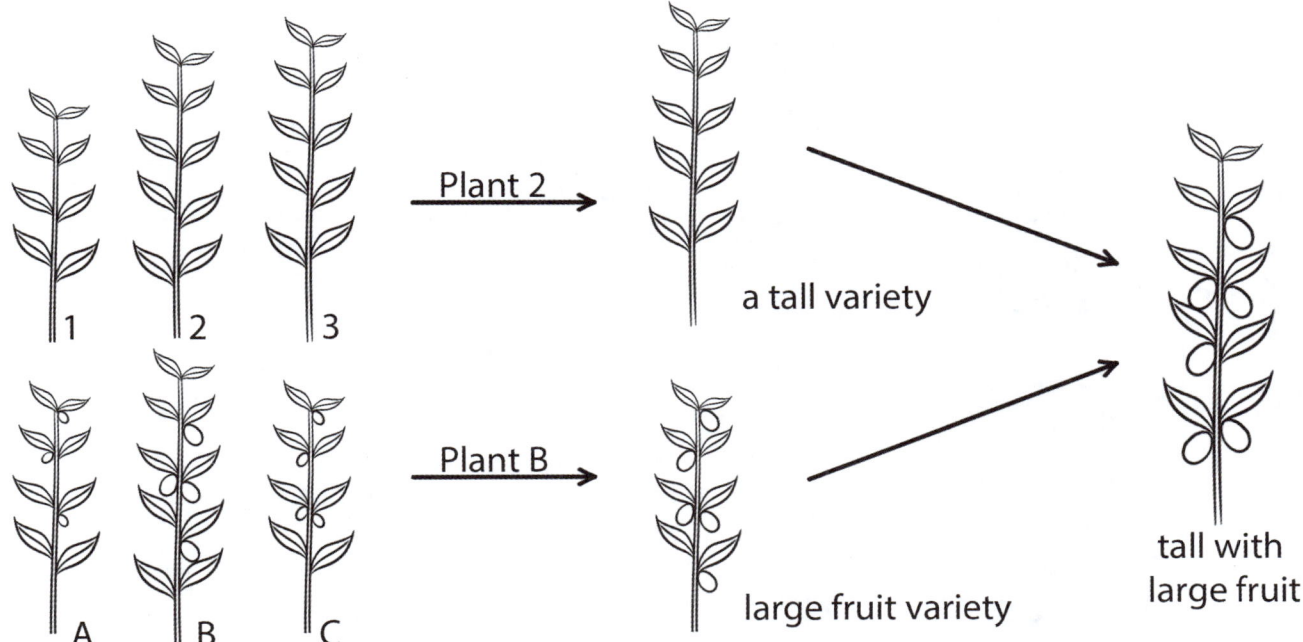

a   Explain how the final plant bred by a farmer, using Plant 2 and Plant B, is tall and has large fruit.

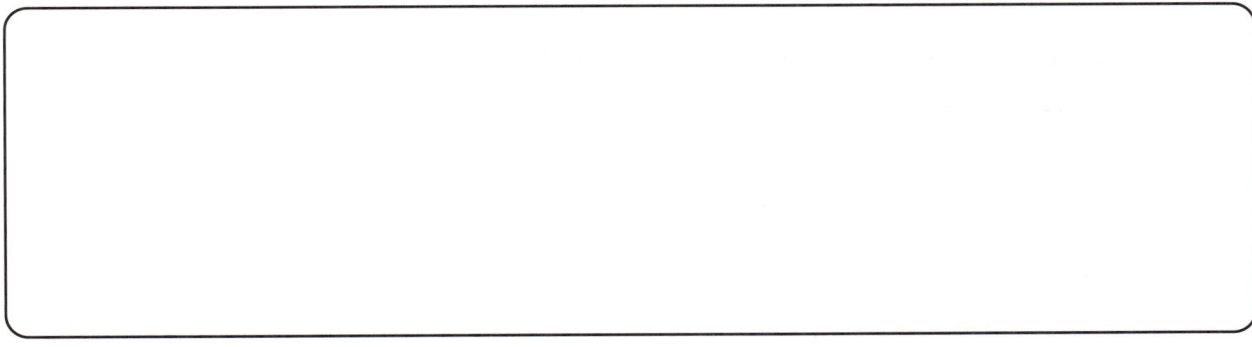

b   Draw the offspring that would be produced if Plant A were pollinated by pollen from Plant 1.

12 a Draw a line to match each beak to the food that the bird is best adapted to eat.

A

B

C

D

E

F

G

nuts

small seeds

small animals

insects buried in mud

small fish

nectar inside flowers

b Which species of bird was not matched to a type food?

c What would happen to this species if it could not move away to find food?